DOGS

The Love They Give Us

A good dog-person match is a gift of the heavens.
　　　　　　　　　　　　　　　　　　—Roger Caras

DOGS
The Love They Give Us

Susan DeVore Williams

Fleming H. Revell
Old Tappan, New Jersey

All Scripture quotations in this book are taken from the King James Version of the Bible.

Library of Congress Cataloging-in-Publication Data

Dogs, the love they give us / [complied by] Susan Devore Williams.
     p.   cm.
   ISBN 0-8007-1585-3
   1. Dogs—literary collections. I. Williams, Susan DeVore.
PN6071.D6D64 1988
636.7'0887—dc 19   88-11118
                                              CIP

Copyright © 1988 by Susan DeVore Williams
Published by the Fleming H. Revell Company
Old Tappan, New Jersey 07675
Printed in the United States of America

This book is for my dad,
Dr. Hugh "Pidge" Williams of Sparta, Wisconsin,
who taught me to care about animals—
and made me love to tell stories as much as he does.

I'm especially indebted to friends—both old and new—whose enthusiasm about this project made my work a little easier. To name them all would be impossible. A few deserve medals: Lee Lofaro of *Guideposts;* Martha Moore; Dr. Michael Fox; Marjorie Holmes; Rebecca and Randy True; Christian veterinary students of the University of California at Davis; Bill Kennedy of Friends of Animals in New York; Dale Walden of the Pet Food Institute in Washington, D.C.; Revell staff and friends and my own family and friends who graciously provided snapshots of their pets; Karen Staps-Walters and the teachers and students of Sacramento Country Day School; Mrs. Jones and her students at Florin Christian Academy of Sacramento; Mrs. Orr and her teachers at Capital Christian School in Sacramento. And an extra big hug for my husband, Richard Kirkham.

"It doesn't count as playing dead if you snore"

Contents

Introduction

First of all, you should know that I am basically a friendly, down-to-earth, conservative kind of woman. If I were a European nation, I'd be Switzerland. If I were a dog, I'd be a cocker spaniel. I've been told I even have a "mainstream" look about me—a distinct advantage at garage sales, where perfect strangers will allow me to pay them by check without any identification.

I can't be accused of being extreme. It takes an awful lot to get me riled. I think I inherited some of that temperament from two Scandinavian grandmothers. It means I'm sort of an eccentric nonpartisan in most discussions: I have definite opinions, but I assume that the next guy's views—if I can get to the heart of them—may well be just as valid as my own. More than one person has been dumbfounded to discover, in the middle of an argument with me, that I'm defending *his* viewpoint more vigorously than my own. It's created a certain amount of confusion, I suppose. In high school I caused a minor stir at the beginning of the debate season when I told the coach I wanted to speak for *both* sides of each question. When she said I had to be either *pro* or *con,* I switched to Interpretive Reading.

I'm so cheerfully open-minded under most circumstances, in fact, that people are often shocked to learn about a couple of areas in my life where I'm capable of transforming myself into a fierce, fiery-eyed, sword-swinging crusader at the drop of a hat. One of those areas—the one that gets me into the most trouble—is where the animals hang out. Not just *my* animals, you understand—*all* animals.

For as long as I can remember, I've acted like the Joan of Arc—I mean *Ark*—of the animal world. I've been known to leap from moving cars to rescue injured dogs and cats, to climb tall trees to replace a fallen chick from a sparrow's nest, and to threaten to break the knees of terrified little boys I've caught in the act of stoning frogs to death in a pond. Once I even challenged a dog-napper who threatened me with a gun as he held a choking dog from a rope in his other hand—and I won! I won't get into it, but I'll admit it gave me trembling spasms in my elbows for a week. It's not easy to be Joan of Ark.

My problems over animals may be genetic. My eighty-two-year-old father, "Pidge" Williams, is an old-fashioned country doctor with a rare gift for storytelling and a profound love and compassion for animals. As a result, many of the stories I remember from my Wisconsin childhood were true-life animal stories that could only come from small-town and rural America.

A few of Dad's old patients still remember the day Dave Jenkins' dog was hit by a car. Dave called Dad right away, asking if he could bring the dog to the clinic to be X-rayed. Dad suggested he take the dog to the town vet, but Dave would have none of that. "I don't want a *vet*," he said. "This is my *dog*, for Pete's sake! I want our family doctor!"

How could Dad refuse such a plea? He agreed to look at the dog, and within a few minutes Dave arrived with the dog. Dad and his nurse met them and the three of them carried the pitiful pooch through the crowded waiting area into an exam room. There, an X ray showed there were no broken bones. The dog lived for some years after that.

That was in the 1940s or '50s the best I can remember, but people still see my dad on the street from time to time and say, "Doc, I remember the day Dave Jenkins carried his dog through your waiting room," and they'll trade stories for a while.

There was also the story about Marv Libke and his plothound. (I never knew what a plothound was, exactly, but there seemed to be a lot of them around our area.) As my dad explained it, Marv loved this dog like a baby. It went everywhere with him, and when Dad went to Marv's house, the dog was always treated like one of the family.

One afternoon while Dad was at the clinic he got a frantic call from Marv. The dog had jumped a fence, he said, and a foot-long reed had run up his leg. Marv had taken him to the vet, but after much probing the vet simply couldn't get it out. Reeds have a structure a lot like a giant foxtail, and when they go in, they grip the flesh like a toggle bolt. Marv begged my dad to come right over to his house and give it one more try.

Naturally, he did. The dog was in a lot of pain, but Dad quickly saw that the reed was not going to come out the way it had gone in. He made an incision a foot above the entry point and managed to pull it out in one piece—all without much pain to the dog. As he held up the bloody reed, he saw that Marv's face was covered with tears. "I never saw him cry, before or after that day," Dad says. The dog recovered without incident, and my dad has always claimed it was one of his most satisfying pieces of surgery.

I heard for years about Dad's childhood animal experiences. His mother died just after he was born, and a few years later, when his father remarried, he was sent off to live with relatives and friends because his stepmother simply didn't want him around. Dad spent summers on the farms of various relatives, and winters with others who agreed to take him in for a time. He adapted well to his itinerant life-style—partly, I'd guess, because most of the places he lived had animals that were a predictable source of affection. One home had a cat that Dad named Tige—short for Tiger. The cat always slept under the covers at the foot of his bed, keeping him warm on cold nights. At another house, a pet squirrel lived in his pocket most of one summer. With all the assorted tame and wild animals he got to know, Dad's often said it's a wonder he didn't die of rabies or mange.

Anyway, I guess I come by my passion for animals honestly. I might as well go ahead and be passionate—after all, if it's genetic, there's nothing I can do about it.

For years of my adult life I worked to help animals on a one-at-a-time basis. Strays seemed to pass the word among themselves that I was an easy mark, and they hunted me down with remarkable persistence. When I lived in Minneapolis, a dog I'd never seen found its way into my office at the University of Minnesota Health Sciences Center and through several closed corridors to my desk, where he immediately put down roots. It was during those years that I became the first person in history to be treated by the University Health Service for a squirrel bite—which was the result of my attempts to hand-feed Planter's Cocktail Peanuts to the little guy who begged at my office window.

In Folsom, California, where I lived for a couple of years on an isolated bluff on the American River, my name must have been scribbled on fire hydrants. Stray dogs found me everywhere—at the grocery store, on the way to church, and even in the parking lot of a laundromat, where a skinny, filthy dog I named Buddy dramatically threw himself in front of my parked car and collapsed.

It was also in Folsom that I got involved with Gordon Brong and his now-famous "Misfit Zoo"—a collection of injured and orphaned animals that could not be returned to the wild and were brought to Gordon one at a time because he was known as a compassionate animal lover. I volunteered for a year or two to help Gordon muck out cages and feed the zoo's population. In exchange, Gordon taught me about the real world of the animals, as opposed to the world I'd read about and experienced in my sheltered existence in cities. It was an experience I'll always treasure—in spite of the fact that I've never quite recovered from being singled out (in a way I'm not allowed to describe in print) as the love object of the zoo's Siberian tiger. As I say, it's not easy to be Joan of Ark.

Through all of this, of course, my own pets have loved me, taught me, encouraged me, and bled me dry. Which is what pets are supposed to do, I guess. They've wrung out my emotions and carried me to the heights and depths the human spirit is capable of surviving—all without a hint of apology. Not that I expected one. Animals tend to become arrogant about their status when they live with me.

Of course, after years of this kind of thing, there was only one thing left for me to do. I had to write a pet book. I've been threatening to do it for years. Only last night I got caught up in an argument with one of my best, most belligerent Christian friends—a gun-toting lawman who likes to say that "God looks at animals the way He looks at rocks and trees—as decorative, but of no value except as food or as labor-saving devices." Clearly there was no convincing him, for he claimed that God had revealed it all to him over coffee and raisin toast while he was reading his Bible. Well, maybe that's not *quite* the way he told it, but you understand what I was dealing with. This man, of course, didn't know he was walking in a mine field as we talked. I like it better when there's no warning.

After the fireworks, while the smoke was still clearing, I was tempted to put an end to his ranting by saying what I've said a hundred times before: "One of these days, I'm going to write something about the spiritual side of animals, and that will settle things." Except this time was different. As my stubborn friend declared that nothing in the world could convince him that animals had any spiritual value, I glanced at the thick manuscript for this book, neatly stacked and almost ready to send to my publisher. It was a great moment. I smiled the secret smile of one who knows how God likes a challenge and said, "We'll see, my friend. We'll see."

—SUSAN DeVORE WILLIAMS

A Man and His Animals

by Dr. James Dobson

"Show me how a man treats his animals, and I'll show you what he thinks of people." That's a proverb with numerous exceptions, of course, but a correlation does exist. Anyone who would care about the welfare of a helpless dog or cat or bird is likely to have a soft spot for hurting people, as well. My dad was such a man. He loved everything God made, especially furry little canines called toy terriers.

Penny was a brilliant representative of that breed. We adopted him into our family when I was thirteen years of age, and the two of us grew up together. By the time I left for college, he was established as a full-fledged member of the Dobson household, with all the rights and privileges thereof. He and my dad had a special understanding for one another, like two old friends who could communicate deep feelings without uttering a word. Only dog lovers will fully comprehend what I mean.

But alas, Penny grew old and decrepit. At seventeen years of age, he was afflicted with a terminal case of cancer and was obviously experiencing severe pain. He would walk the fence and moan hour after hour. My dad knew the time had come to put his little friend to sleep, but he couldn't bring himself to do it.

"How can I kill my dog?" he would ask.

But it was more cruel to let Penny suffer. So Dad made an appointment with the veterinarian at the humane society to discuss the matter. The doctor was a perceptive man and recognized how painful this event was for my father. He shared a similar situation with reference to his own dog, and these two grown men sat and wept together.

The decision was made to end Penny's life, and the day was chosen. Throughout the prior afternoon, a man and a dog sat together under the vine-colored arbor in their back-yard. Neither spoke. (Penny communicated his thoughts with his ears and eyes and tail.) I suspect they both cried. Then they said goodbye for the final time.

When the moment came, Penny was given five barbiturates to prevent him from recognizing the despised smell of the kennel. My mother handed him to the attendant and then hurried back to the car. Dad was visibly shaken. For nearly a week, he sat alone under the arbor, going there immediately after fulfilling his teaching responsibilities at the college each day. He continued to grieve for Penny for seveal years.

During this time, we encouraged my father to get another dog, but he was reluctant to expose himself to another painful loss. Nine years passed before he considered trying to replace the memory of Penny.

But wait, why don't I let him tell you the story in his own words. The following narrative was written by my dad, shortly before his death.

Guaranteed Healthy

I like dogs. Some of my best friends are dogs! I sometimes think that I can communicate better with dogs than I can with people. At least I have never had a dog misunderstand me to the point of breaking up a friendship once it was established! I had grieved for my little toy terrier, Penny, for nine years. I said I would never get another dog. Some of this was due to the Judas Iscariot kind of guilt I was carrying. You see, I was forced by my very love for him to end his hopeless agony. I, his trusted keeper, betrayed him to his executioner! Penny, so gentle, so obedient, so intelligent! Gone was my constant companion of seventeen years! I miss him still and always will but, "nine years is enough," I told my wife. "I will get me another dog."

"You are just asking for more pain," she said. "A dog's life usually averages about eight to ten years—then you will have to go through this sorrow again."

"Maybe not," I said. "I have thought a lot about this

decision. I will soon be over the hill myself. It could be that we will arrive at the Golden Gate at about the same time."

I decided to take great care in selecting this new pet. I wanted the same kind of dog, a toy terrier, but he would have to be pedigreed. Penny had been a lucky accident— a throw-back more like his fox terrier ancestors. I know the breed and know, too, that beyond the A.K.C. papers, you have to select the individual dog for intelligence and other desirable qualities. You have to get a pup by six weeks of age, to be sure he hasn't been ruined by someone else. Then he would have to be in perfect health, having had the necessary shots, etc.

All these thoughts were getting settled in my mind as I started watching the papers for dog advertisements. No luck. Someone would always beat me to the best dogs, since I wouldn't answer an ad on Sunday, and that's when the thoroughbreds are offered. Finally, I saw a notice from a pet shop about a toy terrier, but I didn't take it seriously.

"There's something funny about this," I told my wife. "The ad says the dog is a nine-month-old thoroughbred, but he has no papers. Nine months in a pet shop and nobody wants him! It doesn't sound good to me. I wouldn't buy an unregistered dog anyway!" But later, I said, "Let's just drive out and see him."

We found the shop in a run-down section of the city. My wife was almost afraid to get out of the car. The business was in one room of an old abandoned house. When I stepped through the front door, the stench almost ovewhelmed me. I spotted the dog in question at once. He was crowded into a cubicle with other larger puppies who were bumping him and stepping on his tiny body. They were a motley assortment of mongrels of various kinds, all yapping and defecating; some were trying to sleep away their misery, curled up on the wire bottom of the filthy enclosure

When the saleslady brought the little toy terrier out and put him down on the floor he seemed to be in a wall-eyed trance.

"This dog has been through some traumatic emotional experience," I thought. He looked up at me with pitiful glazed eyes that reflected unspeakable sadness. Far from considering him, I couldn't believe anyone would offer an animal for sale in this condition. His skinny little frame, all four pounds of it, was trembling, and every few seconds he would cough and gag from some kind of chest infection. I thought I recognized this as a case of the dreaded distemper. Between coughs, he would dig frantically at his ears, which were infested with mites. He would follow me about the room, meekly, his tiny tail clamped tightly down—a picture of dejection.

"Nobody knows what other disease he has got—maybe incurable," I thought. "Oh, no! I'm not getting into that!" But in spite of myself I wanted to cry. He seemed to be saying, "You look like a nice man, but I know you will be like all the rest." He was so little and helpless and hopeless. While I was hardening myself to his unhappy fate with such reasoning as "It's not my fault . . . I can't turn my home into a dog hospital," he put out his warm pink tongue and licked my hand, as much as to say, "Thanks, anyway, for coming to see me." I had to get out of there quick!

We were silent as we drove away. When we had gone a few blocks I made an instant decision. I guess it was the effect of that lick on the hand—the intuitive longing it expressed. Wheeling the car around, I started back. I turned stone-deaf to the neatly logical reasoning my wife poured into my ear. In a split second, instead of a nameless wart of a dog in a rotten pet shop, that had become my little dog in there, suffering and lonely and sick! I was bursting with compassion that should rightfully have been extended on a more worthy object: I know, God, please forgive me. I wrote the check and received in exchange a receipt for the money. On it were the incredible words, *Guaranteed Healthy!*

I folded the shivering form into my arms, stink and all. A warm bath soon removed the nauseating smell; then I took him to the best veterinarian I could find. He took one look and shook his head.

"I'll try, but I can't promise he'll make it," he said. It was days of antibiotics for the cough, weeks of application of drops for the ear mites, worm medicine, shots of various kinds, a tonic to regulate that wildly beating little heart, and love made warm by years of grieving for Penny. And to the astonishment of the doctor, most of all, we have a dog to be proud of, fit and sound.

And talk about gratitude! My pup, whom we named

Benji, expresses it in the blasphemous, idolatrous way he worships me. He thinks I am God Almighty when he comes to meet me in the morning, twisting and wiggling like he will tear himself in two. It is as though he will never allow himself to forget his private hell in the pet shop!

Three years from this happy beginning, Benji was to lose his beloved master. He had seen my mother and father leave in the car one morning, but only one of them returned. No one could explain to him the meaning of death, of course. So Benji sat waiting month in and month out, straining to hear the sound of that familiar voice. The shutting of a car door would bring him hope and excitement . . . followed by obvious disappointment. Wrong person, again.

I visited my mother several months after the funeral to help pack my father's possessions and give away his clothes. As I busily folded coats and pants and placed them in a suitcase, Benji jumped on the bed. He reverently approached the clothes and sniffed them carefully on all sides. He climbed into the suitcase and curled up within one of my father's most familiar coats. Then he looked up at me.

"I understand, Benji. I miss him too," I said.

Dr. Dobson is a psychologist, best-selling author, and head of the "Focus on the Family" radio and television ministries.

A recent study at Bloomsbury University has proved that men and women who grow up in families with dogs have significantly higher self-esteem and better interpersonal skills than those who never had dogs as kids.

with organic matter leaning heavily on bones, sparrow carcasses and choice bits from the trash burner. He has even gone into the next county to drag home a cow's skull and mount it in the rock garden off the back porch. His efforts also include protecting our home from visitors by placing both front paws on their shoulders and trying to slobber them to death.

To keep up this pace requires him, of course, to keep up his strength. Which in turn requires him to keep up his appetite. And when Brutus' appetite is up, dry dog food is like peanuts to him, and after a large can of Alpo he will look at you as if he's just had his *hors d'oeuvres*, bring on the entree.

Now, if I'm not too late, let me insert a warning here: If you bring your dog chicken bones for four days straight and think you can come home barehanded on the fifth day with impunity, forget it. Unless, that is, you have a soul encrusted to the point where you can look into a pair of brown eyes large enough to serve as cable-TV dishes and say, "Sorry boy, no chicken bones tonight."

Even if my tender nature had survived this, I'm a pushover when it comes to a dog drooling on my briefcase. And then be began his roll-over trick as soon as he let me into the house. When this didn't produce the chicken, he resorted to his fail-proof gig of bringing the so-called master his slippers. By this time I was trying to hide behind the evening paper. But there's no reading the paper with that long, black nose ramming up under it and those cable-TV dishes staring you right in the face.

Removing my slippers, I put on my shoes, picked up my briefcase, drove to the nearest Kentucky Fried Chicken and pretended to arrive home from work a second time.

You might think that anyone as smart as I am would have learned his lesson, wouldn't you? . . . I say, wouldn't you? Never mind. That Saturday night, however, I compounded my mistake by bringing home a doggie bag containing two steak bones from our night out at Ponderosa. By the quaint way he had of attacking me before attacking them, he let me know that the concept of doggie bags belongs right up there with the fire hydrant and the yew tree. And the reason I dreamed of being swallowed by Jaws that night wouldn't have taken Freud five seconds to interpret.

For our next gastronomic foray out, my wife chose a Chinese restaurant. Instead of standing firm and overruling her, as I've often thought of doing, I stood soft and went along, as usual. Not that I'm allergic to Chinese food—their cuisine just isn't noted for doggie leftovers. This didn't occur to me again until we came home. Until Brutus met us at the door, to be exact, eyes aglow, tail awag, mouth adrool.

Reaching up and patting him on the head, I patiently explained that it wasn't feasible to fetch home a doggie bag *every*time we went out. I told him there would also be days when business luncheons would preclude my brown-bagging the bones from the chicken parts. I even tried to get his feet off my shoulders by opening a can of his favorite cat food. Many a morning we'd seen him nose the cat halfway across the kitchen and beat her back to her dish before he turned to his own rations. Not tonight; no way. Whoever heard of a dog eating cat food?

So, with those accusing brown cable-TV dishes burning into mine as if I'd just signed an agreement to have him sterilized at dawn the next day, on went my shoes, my coat, the ignition, and it was off to ye olde White Tower hamburger shoppe for four with everything but pickles. "A dog that won't eat pickles can't be very hungry," I had once reasoned with Brutus, nearly losing my hand trying to retrieve one he hadn't touched.

The United Way victory dinner the following week was not enjoyed by one and all. One was nearly finished when he realized the committee had not taken Brutus into consideration when planning the menu. So one had tried to act the slob (not a particularly difficult role) by sopping up some gravy with a hard roll and surreptitiously slipping it into his napkin and thence into his pocket. But there is always some nosy dame at these functions who has nothing better to do than look around to see who might be sopping up the gravy with a hard roll, etc. So there went that.

"You go in," I said to Lois as we approached the front door empty-handed, or doggie-bagless, to be precise, "and let me in through the bedroom window. Maybe Brutus will think I've been mugged and taken to the hospital." Which might have been the easy way out, at that.

Many things could be said about Brutus' whine, but No. 1 among the things, it is pervasive. It can pervase the kitchen door, the bedroom door, the bed covers and the pillow. Thus, around 2 A.M. I removed the pillow and covers from my head, climbed out of bed, put on my clothes, pushed the car into the street and drove to the chicken place. The chicken place was closed. An hour later I found an all-night Steak 'n Shake. The hamburgers looked so good I ordered one for myself. Then I made the mistake of going into the house before eating mine. And there went that.

At least I learned my lesson.

Tonight Lois walked over to the theater, only three blocks away. But I took the scenic eight-block route past Pizza Hut to pick up a slab of pepperoni for Brutus. From the craning of necks, its aroma smelled up the theater at least six seats in back, in front and on each side of us. But turning 20 or 30 heads in a darkened theater sure beats driving 30 or 40 blocks in the dark of night looking for a late-night snack for a big-big dog who by that time is in no mood for excuses.

*M*artin Luther said of his little dog Toelpel, "Ah, if I could only pray the way that dog looks at meat!"

Little Dog Found

by Aletha Jane Lindstrom

I saw her first in mid-December during one of Michigan's cruelest winters. She was running across the frozen barnyard, a small ghost of a dog, almost obliterated from sight by swirling snow.

Living in the country, we've become accustomed to seeing abandoned dogs and cats. We seldom see the same one twice, but this one was strangely different. My husband, Andy, and I glimpsed her frequently—in the barnyard, the fields, the woods, along the road. And she was running, always running, head held high, either trying desperately to find someone or fleeing in abject terror.

My heart went out to the small creature. How could she possibly survive the bitter cold? Even Collie, our big farm dog, who loves winter, was content to remain indoors.

But the plight of the little lost dog provided only brief distraction from the black mood that engulfed me. My dad had died recently and it had been hard to let him go. Though I was sustained by God's promise that we'll be reunited with our loved ones, lately there had been dark times when my faith flickered. Could I trust God's promise? The question gnawed at me. For a while I prayed about it, then stopped.

On one below-zero evening, as I walked down the drive for the newspaper, I sensed I was being followed. I looked back, and there was the lost dog—a small beagle with big freckled feet, a wagging tail and soft, pleading eyes. I removed my mitten, but before I could touch her, she cowered and drew back. Then she panicked and fled into the woods, leaving bloody footprints in the snow.

I couldn't sleep that night; the memory of those eyes haunted me. Had she been stolen for hunting and later abandoned? Where was she now? Had she found shelter from the bitter cold, or was she still running, terrified and alone? The next morning we followed tracks in the woods until we found her. Andy held out a piece of meat and she crept toward it on her belly. When she drew close enough, I grabbed her. She struggled and cried until her strength was gone. Then she lay whimpering in my arms.

We wrapped her in a blanket and took her to the vet. "Poor little mutt," I said as we carried her in. "He'll probably have to put her down."

The vet removed the blanket, now bloodstained, and ran gentle, capable hands over the emaciated body. The head, it seemed, was permanently tipped to one side. She was covered with cuts, welts and scars, and the pads were worn from her feet. "She's either been running for days over frozen ground or digging to make a bed in the leaves—probably both," he said.

Silently we awaited the verdict. "She's a good little beagle," he said at last. "I think we can save her." "Then I'd better advertise for the owner," I said.

"I wouldn't bother," the vet replied. "She's smart. If she's from around here, she'd have found her way home—that is, if she'd wanted to go . . ."

"But she's so frightened. How long before she'll get over that?"

"Never—not entirely. Apparently she's been badly abused. When that happens a dog becomes either vicious or afraid for the rest of its life." His voice softened. "And obviously this little dog will never be vicious."

"You mean she'll even be afraid of us?"

"Probably." He was silent for a moment and then added thoughtfully. "But we can't be sure. Sometimes love works wonders."

That night I brought a dog bed from the attic and placed it near the kitchen stove. To my surprise she crept in immediately, settled down with a long sigh and closed her eyes. For the first time the trembling stopped.

I knelt beside her, my mind filled with questions. This small stranger, seemingly from nowhere—why had she approached me in the drive, pleading for affection? And why, needing it so much, had she fled in terror when I offered it? It seemed we had something in common: We were both afraid to trust.

Gently I stroked the soft ears. "You can trust us, Puppy," I whispered. "You needn't be afraid—ever again." I placed an old shawl over her head and tucked it in, making sure it would stay.

"It seems we have ourselves another dog," Andy said the next morning.

I nodded. "I'm not sure I'm happy about it. Now that Tim's away from home, I figured we wouldn't get another dog . . . after Collie. They all die and break your heart sooner or later." *That's the way with love,* I thought, remembering Dad.

"Let's forget the heartaches," Andy said gently, "and remember the happy times. They've given us so many of them."

He was right, of course. I couldn't imagine life without a dog. Besides, I'd already succumbed to this one. She was so hurt and frightened, so little and alone. And she needed us so desperately. Her eyes, her most endearing feature, were dark puddles, reflecting her emotions. I longed to see them shining with eagerness and love—as a little dog's eyes should be.

We continued calling her "Puppy." Somehow it seemed to fit. I remembered what the vet said about fear, but I couldn't believe she'd be afraid of us. She was. She allowed us to minister to her injuries, but when we reached out to pet her, she cringed and pulled away, as if she feared we would strike her. I wondered if perhaps that was why her head was tipped.

We gave up trying to pet her. "She'll come to us when she's ready to trust us," I said. But the rejection hurt. I wondered if that's the way God feels about us when we fail to trust Him.

Andy, unaware of my thoughts, said, "She'll learn. It's a beagle's nature to be happy and affectionate."

"Love casteth out fear," I said, quoting First John 4:18. Here was another of God's promises. Could I believe this one?

Weeks passed and Puppy didn't respond. Collie seemed to be her only security. I usually walked Collie down the lane in late afternoon. When Puppy's paws were healed, she joined us. Sometimes she'd wander off, following a scent. But when she discovered she was alone, she'd race back to Collie.

Those were the good days. There were other, heartbreaking ones when the beagle seemed to be in a trance. She'd wander to the roadside and huddle there, a solitary figure, gazing up and down. I'd send Collie to bring her back. Inside she took to her bed, her eyes confused and unseeing. I'd sit by her and slip my hand under her chin. "Is there someone you love, Puppy? Someone you've been searching for?"

At such times I wished I knew where she'd come from, what she'd experienced. Then, looking at the sad eyes, the ugly scars, I decided I'd rather not know.

By late spring I noticed changes in her behavior. Her trips to the roadside grew fewer, and she waited as impatiently as Collie for our walks. There were times too, when we were petting Collie, that she'd draw close and watch wistfully. And that was the way things remained.

Then one September afternoon I leaned on the back fence, watching our two dogs. They were in the far side of a back field engaged in a recently discovered pastime, chasing grasshoppers. Collie hunted with her eyes, leaping on her prey. Puppy hunted with her nose, snuffling along the ground. Only her waving white-tipped tail was visible above the weeds.

I watched in amusement. The little dog had been with us eight months now, but she was still afraid, still wouldn't come to be petted. Despite our hopes, our prayers, love hadn't worked its magic after all. Yet just having the small dog and knowing she was enjoying life lent pleasure to my days.

Collie saw me and came running. I knelt and put my arms around her, my eyes still on the waving white-tipped tail moving in the maze of weeds. Suddenly Puppy discovered she was alone. She darted in frantic circles until she caught Collie's scent, then she came racing toward us.

When she reached us, she pushed her eager, squirming body between Collie and me. She looked up, her eyes shining with that soft light that comes only from the heart. "Me too!" they plainly said. "Love me too!"

"I do love you, Puppy. I'll always love you," I said, snuggling her close. So love *had* cast out fear, just as the promise says. "It's all right, Dad," I whispered. A gladness was rising in me that I hadn't felt for a long time. I knew then that God is faithful to *all* His promises.

What a Difference a Child Makes

When the Viet Nam war was coming to a close, soldiers who loved the guard dogs that served with them wrote to the Animal Protection Institute because word had come down from the command level that the dogs were to be abandoned in Viet Nam. These dogs had saved countless American lives and many of the soldiers were outraged and saddened. There were humane societies they appealed to who told them nothing could be done. — Who reforms the Pentagon? But API, in perhaps its most famous crusade, set out to save the war dogs—and did. This is how it was done: the schoolchildren of America were rallied on behalf of the soldiers and their dogs. Letters stormed to President Nixon; and to the Secretary of Defense. API followed up the appeals of the children with its own contacts with the authorities. In the long run, after a complicated battle, the Pentagon retreated—the dogs came home. Moral: Don't give up the fight before you start on grounds that the adversary is too big for you. David *did* lick Goliath—and the power of little chldren is a power greater than that of the generals.

—from *Animal Activist's Handbook,* available from the Animal Protection Institute, P.O. Box 22505, Sacramento, California 95822

Photo from the Animal Activist Handbook
by the Animal Protection Institute,
Sacramento, California.

Weird and Wonderful Dogs

by Valerie Porter

GYP, a German shepherd dog owned by Herbert Neff of Knoxville, Tennessee, left home in a huff when the family's second baby was born but returned without fail on Christmas Day for the next ten years.

ROLF was an Airedale from Mannheim, Germany, who understood arithmetic and learned the letters of the alphabet. Using numbers to represent letters, he would tap out messages with his paw. He is said to have predicted an earthquake in 1912, and to have answered a woman who asked what she could do for him by saying, "Wag your tail."

RAGS was part Scottie, part wire-haired terrier. He turned up in Sing Sing prison in 1929 and remained there for 12 years (voluntarily). He performed tricks to cheer up the prisoners but ignored wardens and guards. Scrupulously fair, he attended a different table at mess every day. He was particularly sensitive to depressed prisoners, and spent a whole night with a potential suicide, growling at him to prevent him from hanging himself.

There was a **SPITZ** who acted as a night nurse for her diabetic mistress: she slept at the crook of her arm and woke instantly if her breathing changed indicating a coma. The spitz would immediately go and wake the woman's daughter in the next room.

DOX was a German shepherd dog detective in Italy and as clever as they come—he could untie knots, unload pistols, and remember a wanted man six years after the fugitive had eluded him. He competed in Europe's annual police-dog matches and first won the crown in 1953, successfully defending it for several years against other famous police dogs like REX of Scotland Yard and XORRO of Paris. Dox won four gold medals, twenty-seven silvers, and had seven bullet-wound scars by the time he was 14 years old. Owned and trained by Police Sergeant Giovanni Maimone, he saved a child from being run over by a car, tracked down a lost skier, kept twelve suspects at bay with raised arms until help arrived, caught a burglar after a long chase with one of his legs shattered by a bullet, and was famous for solving crimes all on his own.

Bishop Doane on His Dog

I AM QUITE SURE he thinks that I am God—
Since he is God on whom each one depends
For life, and all things that His bounty sends—
My dear old dog, most constant of all friends;
Not quick to mind, but quicker far than I
To Him whom God I know and own; his eye,
Deep brown and liquid, watches for my nod;
He is more patient underneath the rod
Than I, when God His wise corrections sends.
He looks love at me, deep as words e'er spake;
And from me never crumb nor sup will take
But he wags thanks with his most vocal tail;
And when some crashing noise wakes all his fear,
He is content and quiet, if I am near,
Secure that my protection will prevail.
So, faithful, mindful, thankful, trustful, he
Tells me what I unto my God should be.
                              —George Washington Doane

*H*eaven goes by favour. If it went by merit, you
would stay out and your dog would go in.
                              —Mark Twain

How Old Is Your Dog in Human Years?

For an average, medium-sized dog:
The first year of life is equivalent to about fifteen human years.
A two-year-old dog is like a twenty-four-year-old person.
A three-year-old dog is about twenty-eight.
Starting with the fourth year, every year of a dog's life is equal to about four human years.
   Thus:
   A four-year-old dog is thirty-two in human terms; an eight-year-old is forty-eight; a twelve-year-old is like a sixty-four-year-old person. At fourteen, a dog is seventy-two in human terms. As a rule, bigger dogs have shorter life spans; smaller ones live longer.

The oldest dog in the record books died at the age of twenty-six, which was equivalent to 142 human years. Of dogs that live past the age of seventeen, some 60 percent are mixed breeds.

Belle

by Marjorie Holmes

We all knew our dog was doomed. After three long months in the hospital and three operations, she was getting no better. And it was all my fault. Nobody blamed me, yet I felt so guilty.

"If Belle's got to be put to sleep," I insisted that awful morning of our decision, "I'm the one who should give the order."

In vain they tried to spare me. "Mom, no, you don't have to. I will," a son volunteered, before plunging forlornly off to school. My husband said he'd do it from the office. But I was adamant. I should have tied her up before we took off in our boat to pull those water-skiers. I should have watched out for her. After all, I was driving the boat the day we hit her.

The family was finally out of the house. I paced the floor, struggling for composure. Get it over with. It should be a relief. We'd been debating this so long . . . I strode to the phone at last. "Doctor Mosseller? We've decided the most merciful thing would be to . . . let Belle go."

"Yes. Okay. I think you're right."

I hung up, drew a deep breath, turned the fire higher under the coffeepot. Don't cry any more; you've cried enough. She'll be so much better off. Drink your coffee, read the paper . . . but, *Oh, Belle, forgive me!* New and more terrible tears suddenly blurred the page. I sprang up, appalled. Feeling like an executioner. As if I had just ordered that one of my own children be put to death— or at least a whole era in the life of our family. Even as I raced back to the phone I was crying out loud, "No, no! What have I done?"

This time the circuits were busy. I dialed again and again. Finally the doctor's aide was saying, "I'll see if I can catch him . . ." Then the doctor himself was on the line.

"Stop, wait, don't do it!" I gasped.

In the silence that followed, my heart almost stopped. "You caught me just in time," he said. "Are you sure?"

"Yes. No! . . . Yes, it's got to be done, but wait till tonight, please. At least we can come down and tell her good-bye."

A bit sheepishly I called my husband then—and he agreed. "But let's not say anything more to the kids," he said. "They've accepted it; no use putting them through it all again."

As we drove the 40 miles to the small Virginia town where we had our summer cabin, we reminisced about Belle.

This fat, polka-dotted Dalmatian had been an oddball from puppyhood. Her eyes didn't match—by day, one was blue, one brown, and after dark they lit up like stop lights, red and green. She barked, she shed, she luxuriated on forbidden sofas, raided trash cans and ate everything that didn't eat her first.

And how she loved to swim. She was always first in the car when we headed for the lake, and the first one out, streaking for the water like a jubilant child. The skiers learned to swoop around her eagerly chugging head.

Then we got a new boat—secondhand boat, rather—but bigger and more powerful than our last. The teen-agers wanted to try it out that evening; I said I'd drive. I had a strange feeling I really ought to tie Belle up. But, sensing excitement, she was already dashing past us. We heard the usual big splash as she dived in.

I forgot all about her. It was enough just to concentrate on the controls, to watch and listen for the signals from my husband and the tensely waiting skiers.

"Hit it!" The traditional call from skiers ready to take off.

I pulled the lever, we shot through the water . . . then that body-shattering jolt. That awful thud. Those wild, agonized yelps.

The details of that dreadful night came back to me so clearly. Our frantic calls to the vets until we reached one who would see her if we'd bring her in. But we'd have to detour, we were told—there was a parade. Then the dash through the countryside, a daughter driving while the rest of us cradled and tried to comfort the blanket-wrapped bundle in the back of the station wagon. Despite the long bumpy detour, we ran into the parade. Our daughter jumped out, dripping wet, and begged a policeman to let us through. He shook his head and turned his back. More desperate miles, only to encounter more parade.

The car stopped. "Here, Daddy, you drive." Again Melanie leaped from the car, and extending both arms, simply stopped the parade until we could pass.

Doctor Mosseller couldn't give us much hope. "I'll try to make her comfortable. If she makes it till morning we may be able to operate, but even then . . ."

Belle made it all through the summer, while that brilliant young vet put her mangled body back together. But one leg refused to heal. More operations loomed—a bone graft, perhaps, but even that would be arduous and doubtful. Amputation would probably be best. We winced at the prospect. Poor Belle—could she stand it? Could we?

Then we were at the vet's office. We could hear Belle barking clear down the corridor, as if she sensed our presence. They wheeled her out on a little cart—and her tail was wagging! Wildly, eagerly, despite the cast and bandages, she greeted us, quivering, contorting in an ecstatic frenzy. People have words to express love; dogs can only strain and wag and frantically lick your hands.

We knew we couldn't put her away. And the doctor could read the message in the tears that ran down our faces. "Look, if you're willing to nurse her, why not take her home until you're sure?"

Rejoicing, we lifted her into the car.

The youngsters couldn't believe it. The dead restored. They were beside themselves. They helped with the nursing—and the spoiling. For she was queen of the family now, reigning from the once-forbidden sofa, this former, often scolded renegade. But we knew we had only postponed the inevitable, and it haunted us. Especially the weekend we took her to the lake, and she lay whimpering, gazing toward the water.

It was at that point I remembered the words in the Bible, "Where two or three are gathered together . . ." (Matthew 18:20). Why not try prayer? My column *Love and Laughter* was appearing in the *Washington Star*. I would ask not only our church and our friends but my readers also to gather in a common spiritual purpose. And so I told the story of Belle, concluding: "The verdict is this. In another month, if the hip has not healed—amputation, or the end. There are no accounts in Scripture of the healing of animals. But I believe the Good Shepherd would have healed a pet had He been asked."

The newspaper was scarcely on the street when the telephone began to ring. Prayer circles. Animal shelters. Individuals. Then came the avalanche of mail.

"The Lord is concerned about everything that is dear to us," one letter said. "He knows every sparrow that falls," another wrote. People shared their experiences, funny and sad. They advised, told of successful amputations. Above all, they told us they were praying.

As for Belle, had she any idea of the floods of love she had released? We can never know. We know only that as she stretched and scrambled around, she became less awkward with the cast, then surprisingly nimble. Two weeks later, when we went back to the doctor, he was amazed. "There's still a lot of damage. The pin has shifted . . . but the tissue is growing!" By the third week he was able to lessen the bindings, by the fourth to remove the cast altogether.

"It's remarkable," he said. "She'll have some arthritis, but she'll be swimming again next summer. This dog is well!"

Belle lived three more years. Still battle-scarred, a little gimpy. And as she would stand, her hips in perfect alignment, I remembered what one reader urged. "Never offer God a picture of injury. Visualize perfection."

And with the living proof of that philosophy before me, I sometimes thought, *Maybe if we all visualized perfection and kept the image vivid, our lives and the whole world would be more perfect.* And if all of us would pray for each other with the selfless warmth and enthusiasm with which people prayed for Belle, miracles could occur every day.

The Power of the Dog

There is sorrow enough in the natural way
From men and women to fill our day;
And when we are certain of sorrow in store,
Why do we always arrange for more?
Brothers and Sisters, I bid you beware
Of giving your heart to a dog to tear.

Buy a pup and your money will buy
Love unflinching that cannot lie—
Perfect passion and worship fed
By a kick in the ribs or a pat on the head.
Nevertheless it is hardly fair
To risk your heart for a dog to tear.

When the fourteen years which Nature permits
Are closing in asthma, or tumour, or fits,
And the vet's unspoken prescription runs
To lethal chambers or loaded guns,
Then you will find—it's your own affair—
But . . . you've given your heart to a dog to tear.

When the body that lived at your single will,
With its whimper of welcome, is stilled (how still!)
When the spirit that answered your every mood
Is gone—wherever it goes—for good,
You will discover how much you care,
And will give your heart to a dog to tear.

We've sorrow enough in the natural way,
When it comes to burying Christian clay.
Our loves are not given, but only lent,
At compound interest of cent per cent.
Though it is not always the case, I believe,
That the longer we've kept 'em, the more do we grieve:
For, when debts are payable, right or wrong,
A short-time loan is as bad as a long.
So why in Heaven (before we are there)
Should we give our hearts to a dog to tear?

—Rudyard Kipling

The Legendary Hachiko

by Byron G. Weis

Every year, a serious and solemn ceremony takes place at the Shibuya railroad station in Tokyo, Japan. Hundreds of dog lovers appear and pay homage to the memory of Hachiko, an Akita dog belonging to Dr. Eisaburo Ueno, who taught at Tokyo University.

Every morning, the faithful dog would walk with his master to the railroad station, and Dr. Ueno would get on the train for the university. Each afternoon, the Akita would come to the station just before the train came in. He would wait, greet his master, and walk home with him. Then one May evening in 1925 Dr. Ueno did not step off the train to greet his dog. He had suffered a heart attack at the university and died. The dog waited until midnight for his master's return, and every evening until his death nine years later, the dog came to the station and awaited

the doctor's return. There was no way to stop the dog or dissuade him from his vigil. It was not until the dog's own death in March 1934 that his presence was missed at the station.

The fidelity of Hachiko was known throughout Japan, and on his death, newspaper stories carried the tale all over the world. Contributions poured in, and a statue was created to the memory of the loyal animal, who throughout his life kept the memory of his dead master alive in his heart.

—from *Animal Heroes*

Only a Dog

(Epitaph from a tombstone in a pet cemetery)

Only a dog, but such love he gave
Cannot have perished in the grave.
So constant and faithful and true a heart
Must in eternity have some part.
And sometimes I fancy
When I've crossed life's sea
I'll find him waiting to welcome me.

A Dog by Any Other Name . . .

The most popular name for a dog is Pepper, according to a survey of over seven thousand pet owners by the Anderson Animal Shelter in South Elgin, Illinois.

After that, favorite names include (in order) Brandy, Lady, Bear, and Rocky. Not unexpectedly, more than half of the dogs had "people names": Sandy, Tiffany, Maggie, Mandy, Heidi, Barney, and Charlie. Others that appeared frequently were Monroe, Dillon, Murphy, McTavish, and Johnson. Even human nicknames were used—Butch, Ace, Corky, Skip, Buddy, and Mac were frequent choices.

There seemed to be a growing number of dogs with initials instead of names—PD and JD were the most popular. (Cats with initials were most often AJ and BJ, but nobody explained these choices.)

Hungry owners—perhaps those on diets—named their dogs after food: Cupcake, Taffy, Pudding, Twinkie, Peaches, and Cookie. There were even several Jelly Beans, presumably in honor of President Reagan.

A large number of dogs were named for TV and movie characters—like Benji, Lassie, Yoda, Darth Vader, and Chewbacca. Some owners had royal aspirations (at least for their dogs), naming them Prince, Duke, Queen, and King. Others stuck to American luminaries like Herbert Hoover and George Washington.

Many owners named their dogs after other animals: Grizzly, Eagle, Wolf. Others apparently named their pets while they were puppies—before they were able to assess the extent of their full growth. Several huge dogs were named PeeWee, Peanut, and Little Bit. Owners' senses of humor surfaced as well: One Chihuahua was named Brutus while a Lhasa Apso was called Moose.

Some names clearly had private significance. One owner offered no explanation of why his Great Dane was named Nosebag.

Half a Dog High

by Byron K. Elliott

Everyone knew that Chauncy was a dog—everyone but Chauncy, that is. He wanted to be something, so he equated himself with the most impressive creature who happened to be present—usually a human, but on occasion a horse or, more frequently, a much larger dog. Most dogs were larger, for Chauncy was a dachshund.

Dachshunds are small dogs, but that didn't bother Chauncy, since he didn't know it. Small as he was, he took enormous responsibility—for his family, for their house, and for the surrounding eight acres of woods, fields, gardens, and lawn, including the chicken coop, where a dozen white leghorns were generally busy kicking the straw around, feeding from the hoppers, and laying nearly a dozen fresh eggs every day. He knew it was up to him to defend the coop from cats, raccoons, and other dogs and to handle the animal life around his home.

Among the animals, woodchucks were by far the most destructive. Chauncy spent long days sniffing around the yard and knew where all their burrows were—quite an achievement, for two of three burrows were always concealed or camouflaged.

Not until I observed an incident from the rooftop of the garage did I realize the science and skill the little dog used in stalking these garden predators.

As I sat on the roof with a .22 rifle, I watched a large woodchuck nibble his way across a field—a bit of clover here and a succulent sprout there—and waited for him to come into better range. On a knoll at the edge of the field, Chauncy was apparently enjoying a nap in the warm sunshine. Then I saw his head move slightly and knew that he too was watching the woodchuck. He suddenly sprang up, barked in the high hunting note used for pursuit, and dashed into the field as fast he his crooked little legs would carry him. Alerted to danger, the woodchuck turned and ran for home. From atop the garage I could see that Chauncy was not running toward the chuck, but instead toward an interception point the chuck would have to cross in flight to any one of his holes. There Chauncy nailed him.

It would have been nice if Chauncy had left all his trophies where he caught them, but he was entitled to boast a bit. He would drag them up to the house and leave them on the threshold for all to see—one just had to be careful in leaving the house not to step on a carcass. He did go too far once, when he pulled a skunk from its hole and dragged it across the field to the front step—just as we were expecting guests for dinner.

One Sunday afternoon the family was out on the terrace. Chauncy flashed out of the woods, around the house, and over to his mistress. As he tugged at her skirt, she understood his message and followed him to the other side of the house, where she saw a fire just starting in the woods. Some children had been playing with matches.

If left alone by the children's playpen, Chauncy would not leave. He would bark if anyone came near or even if a large bird flew overhead. On several occasions he called for help after a spider managed to get inside the pen.

His responsibility for the family was limitless. He checked up on every member of the household the first thing each morning. If he noticed an empty seat at the breakfast table, he would trot up to that person's room and return to query us with a worried look if the missingone were not found. Nature had supplied him with an ample hide that fell easily into wrinkles, especially on his forehead. He had the most eloquent frown in the neighborhood. When he worried, which he did frequently, he worried all over, on the outside as well as internally.

Years later, while the children were away at school, Chauncy extended his patrols to the entire neighborhood. Everyone knew him; he would stop at several doors, wait for a pat on the head, and, concluding that all was well, proceed to the next house. He collected an average of two dozen pats a day.

Sometimes he patrolled the neighborhood with four or five other dogs. His small, crooked legs placed him at the rear of the sniffing column—but then, that is the proper location for the general in command.

In his relationship with other dogs, Chauncy was rarely belligerent. After an introductory sniff for identification purposes, he just ignored them, except that his gait became a swagger in their presence. The only exception was the shepherd that lived down by the river. Some sort of disagreement arose, and Chauncy came home with his hide badly ripped across his shoul-

ders. Our vet sewed him up so neatly that he paid the shepherd another call, which necessitated another visit to the vet. After a third visit the vet refused to sew him up any more. But we heard nothing more of the shepherd. Rumor was the rival had suffered a nervous breakdown.

Our children used to claim that Chauncy was a police dog. If someone said he didn't look like a police dog, they maintained that he was in the Secret Service and must be disguised.

Chauncy was a sensitive little fellow, who showed his feelings in his eyes, his posture, and his movements. He did not like to be called "little wagon train" by the children or to be referred to as "a half-dog high and a dog-and-a-half long"; his hurt feelings were visible in his eyes and lowered head. He seemed pleased when the children recited their favorite dachshund poem:

> "There was a dachshund once, *so* long
> He hadn't any notion
> How long it took to notify
> His tail of his emotion;
> And so it happened, while his eyes
> Were filled with woe and sadness
> His little tail went wagging on
> Because of previous gladness."

Upon hearing this, he would walk over to the nearest family member (usually his mistress), settle down, rest his chin on her toe, and listen. Maybe he liked the cadence, or the rhymes, or the attention suddenly focused on him. Perhaps he understood every word.

Chauncy was a little guy, but he was large in the memories of his family and neighbors. Few of them ever knew that his real name was Lothar, as registered in the American Kennel Club, or that his lineage was aristocratic. They did not doubt that he had been an influential dog in more ways than one, for many of the neighborhood puppies born during his heyday had features at least suggesting a dachshund had put in an appearance.

What to Do When Your Dog Gets Arthritis

Arthritis is just as painful for dogs as it is for humans. Your vet will diagnose the problem, but you'll be able to tell when your dog is arthritic by the way he moves. He just won't seem to get around as well as he used to. Beyond the medicines available to treat arthritis in animals, here are a few ways you can help your dog with the problem:

1. Moderate exercise is good, but avoid overdoing it. Joints will stiffen if your dog avoids walking and moving around. Don't run with an arthritic dog unless he seems eager.

2. Massages ease the pain and can cause some dogs to swoon with ecstasy. Sit next to your dog and begin by massaging the paws. Then move to the wrist joints and on up the legs, one at a time, to the shoulders and hip joints. Finish off with a gentle massage of the back, neck, and head. Warning: Your dog may become addicted to this activity, and may give you no rest until you have massaged him each day.

3. Heat can help, too. Specially wired low-level pet heating pads are available from mail order houses and large pet supply stores. *Don't* use a "people" heating pad, which can overheat and cause burns or fire. It also can give your pet an electric shock if he nibbles the cord or gets the pad damp. Pet heating pads are made to withstand constant use, and are insulated to be wet-proof and hazard-free.

4. Wooly pet pads (made from the same heavy wool as the thick "sheepskin" mattress pads being sold to people) are excellent for an arthritic dog (or any pet). They "breathe," allowing air to circulate around and under the dog, and they offer soft, snuggly comfort to aching bones. Be sure your dog has a warm place to sleep that's away from drafts and dampness.

5. Waterbeds for pets are sold at many large pet supply stores, and they can be very helpful. They're easy to clean and are nonallergenic.

6. Be sure your arthritic dog is getting all the vitamins and minerals he needs. In older dogs, supplements can be helpful. Your veterinarian can supply the right dosage, or suggest where you can find it.

Lord Byron's Dog

A large monument was built at Newstead Abbey to honor Boatswain, Lord Byron's Newfoundland dog. Here is the inscription, written by Byron himself:

Near this spot
Are deposited the Remains
of one
Who possessed Beauty
Without Vanity,
Strength without Ferocity
And all the Virtues of Man
Without his Vices.

This Praise which would be unmeaning flattery
If inscribed over Human Ashes,
Is but a just tribute to the Memory of
"Boatswain," a Dog
Who was born at Newfoundland,
May, 1803,
And died at Newstead Abbey,
November 18, 1808.

When some proud son of man returns to earth,
Unknown to glory, but upheld by birth,
The sculptor's art exhausts the pomp of woe,
And storied urns record who rests below;
When all is done, upon the tomb is seen,
Not what he was, but what he should have been;
But the poor dog, in life the firmest friend,
The first to welcome, foremost to defend,
Whose honest heart is still his master's own,
Who labours, fights, lives, breathes for him alone,
Unhonoured falls, unnoticed all his worth,
Denied in heaven the soul he held on earth;
While man, vain insect! hopes to be forgiven,
And claims himself a sole exclusive heaven.
Oh man! thou feeble tenant of an hour,
Who knows thee well must quit thee with disgust,

Degraded mass of animated dust!
Thy love is lust, thy friendship all a cheat,
Thy smiles hypocrisy, thy words deceit!
By nature vile, ennobled but by name,
Each kindred brute might bid thee blush for shame.
Ye! who perchance behold this simple urn,
Pass on—it honours none you wish to mourn.
To mark a friend's remains these stones arise;
I never knew but one—and here he lies.

How to Find a Lost Dog

The biggest reason dogs get lost is that owners allow them to roam free regardless of strict leash laws in almost every community. In smaller communities this isn't as much of a problem as it is in cities and densely populated suburbs. Free-roaming dogs can fall prey to all kinds of hazards. Dog-napping by unscrupulous dealers who make a living selling animals for laboratory research has become commonplace. Valuable dogs and exotic breeds are sometimes stolen because they'll bring a high price through a newspaper ad.

Dogs occasionally simply can't find the way home—usually after fresh snow has covered up a familiar trail or rain has eradicated the scents normally used for direction. Dogs frequently get lost when the family moves to a new area. They need several weeks—or even months—to familiarize themselves with all the new scents and sights. Some dogs are "fence-jumpers," and others get out of their yards from time to time while the family is away. Lost dogs may wander until they're picked up by caring people or by the city pound. Unless your dog has an ID tag and is licensed, it may be impossible for those who take him in to trace his ownership.

Tatooing offers some protection against dog-nappers. (But remember—some research labs don't bother to carefully inspect the animals they buy, so they can miss the tatoo.) Several national dog registries serve as clearinghouses for reports of lost pets once they've been tatooed and registered. A small fee is charged. Ask your veterinarian about it. He'll tatoo your Social Security number on your dog's inner right hind leg.

Most lost dogs turn up within a ten- to twelve-mile radius of the place they were last seen. Your best chance of finding the dog is within the first week after he's disappeared. Organize your search:

1. Immediately put an ad in the newspaper under "lost animals." Give a clear description and offer a reward, if possible, for his safe return. And don't forget to check the "found" ads every day. Also read the "pets for sale" ads and call any that could describe your dog—without giving away the fact that your dog

is lost. Ask for a brief description of the dog being advertised, and if it seems possible it's your dog, take someone with you and *immediately* go to look at the dog. Above all, don't give the person on the phone *any* inkling that you suspect this may be your dog. If you do, don't be surprised if the dog has mysteriously vanished by the time you arrive.

2. Scour your neighborhood—especially any parks, wild areas, rivers, creeks, or woods where your dog might have wandered in search of a good time. Dog collars can get caught on fences or branches, and dogs are trapped until humans happen along to free them.

3. Call all the neighborhood families to have them watch for your dog. Ask them to have their kids keep their eyes peeled, too.

4. Have a leaflet printed at an instant-printing shop with a photo or good sketch of your dog. Give his name, age, and physical description, along with phone numbers where you can be reached twenty-four hours a day. Take the leaflet to grocery stores, shopping malls, and neighborhood hangouts. Ask managers if you can tape the leaflet to windows. (Don't forget to return and take them down when the dog is found.)

5. Call the principals of all the area schools. Ask them to tell students about your dog over the PA system, or leave enough leaflets for each teacher to use in class. Personally ask any teachers you know to make an announcement in class about the dog.

6. Talk with every veterinary clinic and hospital in the area, particularly if your dog has any medical problems. Leave his description with them and a photo, if possible. Those who take him in may need to get him to a vet.

7. Ask a local radio station to give the dog's description over the air (along with your phone number and name). Some local call-in shows will allow owners to do it themselves.

8. Call the local pound *daily for at least a month*. Ask if any dog even vaguely resembling yours has been brought in. If there's the slightest doubt, go there in person. Pounds vary in their policies, but many that have no room for new animals will only give an owner a few hours to claim his pet before it's killed or sold to a laboratory for research. If you miss a day, you may miss your dog—permanently. Pounds usually try to notify owners if dogs are wearing tags or licenses, but collars and tags can be lost as a dog wanders in search of home.

9. Call the local humane society and animal shelters in the area. Strays are often dropped off there. Call them every day.

10. If you live near a corporation or research facility that conducts animal experiments, go there in person every few days and ask to see the dogs that have been bought for laboratory experimentation. Some will cooperate; others will not, fearing lawsuits and "hassles." Be as pleasant as you can and avoid angry confrontations. Most university medical centers and veterinary campuses have large animal research facilities, and they're usually fairly cooperative in checking the animals that are brought to them each day if a pet owner calls to remind them of the pet's description. If any research facility puts you off by saying, "Your pet can't be here—we only buy from licensed dealers," explain to them that many licensed dealers pick up strays that are lost pets like yours. (Don't accuse the facility of buying pets from dog-nappers or unscrupulous dealers; it will only slam the door in your face.)

11. Pray. Call everyone you know, including your church family, and ask them to pray with you that your dog will be found.

I Just Want Kate to Get Well

by Phyllis Hobe

Even before I took Kate, my big, beautiful German shepherd, to the veterinarian, I knew she was in great trouble. She had been limping. At first I thought she'd hurt her leg playing ball, which she loves to do. But the limp came and went, and on rainy days Kate could barely get around.

"She has dysplasia in her left hip," Dr. Gulliford said, shaking his head sadly. He fastened a large X-ray to a light screen. "There," he said, pointing to the place where the top of the leg bone fitted into the hip joint. "You can see why she's in pain every time she takes a step."

The top of the leg bone, which should have been round and smooth, was knobby. Calcium deposits had made it larger than it should have been. Instead of moving comfortably in the hip joint, the leg bone was grinding against it. I winced, imagining how it must have hurt. Yet Kate had never complained. She was always eager for a hike, a swim or a ball game. It was as if she didn't want to worry me. She's that kind of dog.

But I *was* worried. Terribly. Dysplasia is an ugly word to dog owners; it's common in large dogs. I knew of so many dogs whose lives had been cut short by it—and dog owners whose eyes filled with tears as they recalled putting a dog to sleep to end its suffering.

"But Kate's only four years old!" I protested.

"It happens to young dogs, too," Dr. Gulliford said.

To understand how I felt, you have to know what Kate means to me. She's not a pet; she's a companion. I'm a writer and I live alone. As I move through my house, Kate is always with me. When I'm at my desk, she's under it. I'm not a natural athlete, but she's taught me what a treat the outdoors can be. She likes nothing better than welcoming friends to our home—and when my friends invite me to dinner, they almost always invite her, too. My neighbors' children come over to play with her. She also makes it possible for me to live in the country—which is important to me—without feeling lonely or afraid.

I was so sickened by the possibility of losing Kate that it was

hard for me to understand what Dr. Gulliford was saying. He was telling me about a new surgical procedure that would eliminate the pain. It's called arthroplasty, he said. He could refer me to an excellent orthopedic veterinary surgeon. The degree of Kate's recovery, however, would depend on a long period of postoperative therapy. "That's where you come in," he explained. "That'll be your job. But there's a good chance that Kate can return to an active, happy life."

"A good chance" wasn't good enough. I wanted a guarantee. And I wanted it right away, without putting Kate through surgery. You can't tell a dog, "You're going to be all right in a couple of months." Animals only understand the here and now, so any form of hospitalization confuses and frightens them.

I panicked. All the way home I prayed, "Please, Lord, heal my crippled dog." I believed so passionately that He could do it that for the next few days I watched closely for signs that Kate's limp was disappearing. I honestly expected a sudden, dramatic recovery—I thought that was the way God would do it.

Then I realized I had no right to tell God how to do anything. "I know nothing about healing, Lord. I'll leave that to You. I just want Kate to get well, and I'll do whatever You think is best. We all will." Kate put her head in my lap, a signal for me to scratch her ears. Her limp was worse. I made an appointment with Dr. Lynne Maletz, the orthopedic veterinary surgeon recommended by Dr. Gulliford to do the operation.

"She's a good candidate for arthroplasty," Dr. Maletz said after examining Kate and the X-ray. "Your job after the surgery will be to walk Kate very slowly on a short leash several times a day. Gradually she'll begin to use the leg we worked on."

Two days later Kate was home, still a bit groggy from the anesthesia. Her entire left leg was shaved down to the skin, and a stitched, eight-inch incision glared from her hip. She got around on three legs, the fourth swinging loosely and not touching the ground.

She was weak and slept a lot. She was thin too, and I couldn't get her to eat. Even ground beef didn't appeal to her, and day by day she got weaker. One evening when my stepfather called to find out how she was, I broke down. "I'm scared, Dad," I wept. "She can just about stand up—what'll I do when she can't?"

"Scrambled eggs," my dad said. "She loves scrambled eggs! Have you tried that?"

"No—but I will!"

I scrambled two eggs and let them cool. Then I crouched down next to Kate's bed, propped her up against me and brought the bowl to her mouth. Nothing. I held the bowl there, waiting for her dry nose to catch the scent of the food. Suddenly she raised her head and plunged her snout into the bowl. The eggs disappeared. I made, and she ate, three more portions that night. Kate grew stronger before my eyes. The next day I did what my mother would have done for me: I made her a pot of chicken soup and she ate it all. The day after that, she was back on her regular diet and starting to fill out.

Now it was time for me to start Kate's walking therapy. "There'll be no further possibility of dysplasia because we removed the damaged top of the leg bone," Dr. Maletz had explained. "We've made her a new hip socket out of muscle and cartilage, so that'll feel strange for a while. Figure on six to eight weeks before she puts full weight on that leg."

Two weeks went by, but instead of beginning to use the dangling leg, Kate was getting around fairly well on three legs. She refused to put weight on the fourth. The muscles in the dangling leg were starting to atrophy.

I knew what the problem was. German shepherds are known for intelligence; during our slow walks Kate had time to figure out how to avoid putting her left hind foot on the ground. Off the leash she scampered around like a kangaroo, willing to make the best of what she had. But that left leg was getting skinny, and it was always cold as ice.

I panicked again. Was there to be no healing? Was the operation a success and the patient still crippled? Kate's recovery was in my hands now, and I didn't know what to do. "Help me, Lord!" I prayed, leading Kate in our slow walk that was getting us nowhere.

Then I remembered Bill McGlinchey, the trainer who had taught me how to handle my large, rambunctious, powerful dog when she was younger. He knew so much about animal behavior; maybe he could come up with a solution.

He did. "Remember what I told you in our first lesson?" he said. "You have to work her fast; don't give her time to think. Try walking her at a fast trot. Let her get tired from using only one hind leg. Then, when she puts the other foot down, give her a lot of encouragement. Try some sharp right and left turns, too."

It was a cold day, but we went out and put Bill's advice to work. I hated to force Kate to run so hard, and she tired quickly. But she looked up at me, her tongue hanging out the side of her mouth, and I saw trust in her eyes. We kept running until my lungs were numbed by the cold air. And then I saw it. The left hind foot came down. Just a little, the toes scraping the road surface.

"Thank You, Lord!" I whispered. And as I did, I realized that healing is far more complicated than I expected it to be. It isn't God stepping into our world and wiping out all our problems with a wave of His mighty hand. It is God bringing together enough of us to solve our problems with the talents, the insights, the dedication, patience and determination that He has already given to us. It is God's love motivating us to do what we didn't know we could do, to remember what we thought we had forgotten, to call upon others for the skills we ourselves don't possess.

Kate is fully recovered now and as active as ever. She'll always walk with a slight limp because one hind leg is shorter than the other, but you wouldn't notice it unless I told you. And she has no pain—because God brought together everything she needed to get well: the talents and training of her doctors, my stepfather's good memory, the training with Bill McGlinchey long before Kate ever began to limp, and, in spite of my lopsided way of expressing it, my belief in Christ's compassion.

Now, I call that a healing.

Puttin' on the Dog

Barney Rybka became famous recently when he appeared in the wedding of Raymond and Lee Ann Rybka of Ohio. The Rybkas wrote to *Dog Fancy* magazine to describe the event. Explaining that both of them are animal lovers, the Rybkas naturally decided to include Barney, their golden cocker spaniel, in the formal ceremony. Dressed in a doggy tuxedo and top hat ordered from a mail-order catalog, Barney comported himself with all the dignity the occasion warranted. Although there was a best man, Barney was officially designated "best dog" and sat quietly through the entire ceremony at the best man's side. The dog, who had been with Raymond for eleven years before the wedding, has taken Lee Ann into his heart, and the three of them have become one big, happy family.

A faithful friend is a strong defense: and he who hath found such a one hath found a treasure.
                                        —from the Apocrypha

Histories are more full of examples of the fidelity of dogs than of friends.
                                        —Alexander Pope

Recollect that the Almighty, who gave the dog to be companion of our pleasures and our toils, hath invested him with a nature noble and incapable of deceit.
                                        —Sir Walter Scott,
                                        from The Talisman

The Many Faces of Maxi

Happy Easter!

Boo!

Merry Christmas!

Here comes the
BRIDE . . . + THE GROOM!

MAXI AS HERSELF

*Maxie lives in New Jersey
with Norma and Tricia Chi-
mento. She is costumed and
photographed by Tricia.*

Small Dogs

Have you ever tried to hold a Great Dane?
Lifting a large dog would be really insane.
And even though many questions may rise,
I think that a small dog is just the right size.
Lovable, furry, and cuddly too,
It's interesting to watch the things that they do.

Chewing your shoes, and spreading the trash

It's enough to cause your emotions to clash.

Lovable companions for everyday life,
For brother, for sister, for husband and wife.
Whether Pekingese, Poodle, Chihuahua or Pug,
Small dogs are cute, and tempting to hug.

—Shane Raynor, Age 13,
North Carolina

Coming Home

by David Redding

I remember coming home from the navy after World War II. Home was so far out in the country that when we went hunting, we had to go toward town. We had moved there for my father's health when I was thirteen. We raised cattle and horses.

That is how I got Teddy, a big, black Scottish shepherd. Teddy was my dog, and he would do anything for me. He waited for me to come home from school. He slept beside me, and when I whistled he ran to me even if he were eating. At night no one would get within half a mile without Teddy's permission. During those long summers in the fields I would only see the family at night, but Teddy was with me all the time. And so when I went away to war, I did not know how to leave him. How do you explain to someone who loves you that you are leaving him and will not be chasing woodchucks with him tomorrow as always?

So, coming home from the navy that first time was something I can scarcely describe. The last bus stop was fourteen miles from the farm. I got off there that night about eleven o'clock and walked the rest of the way home. It was two or three in the morning before I was within half a mile of the house. It was pitch dark, but I knew every step of the way. Suddenly Teddy heard me and began his warning barking. Then I whistled—only once. The barking stopped. There was a yelp of recognition, and I knew that a big black form was hurtling toward me in the darkness. Almost immediately he was there in my arms. To this day, that is the best way I can explain what I mean by "coming home."

What comes home to me now is the eloquence with which that unforgettable memory speaks to me of God. If my dog, without any explanation, would love me and run to take me back after all that time, would not my God?

—from *The Golden String*

Church-Going Dogs

by Valerie Porter

In the 14th century, nuns in Romsey often took hounds and other pets with them into church services. William of Wykeham had to reprove them, saying, "We have convinced ourselves by clear proof that some of the nuns bring with them to church birds, rabbits, hounds and suchlike things, whereunto they give more heed than to the offices of the church."

The Bishop of Gloucester was officiating at a service at the Abbey Church in Bath one Sunday with the usual assortment of medieval dogs in attendance. Some of them were turnspit mongrels, accompanying their cooks. (Turnspit dogs were harnessed to wheels and trained to walk in circles so the spits on which meats were roasted were kept turning continuously.) The lesson was from Ezekiel, and it included the words, "As if a wheel had been in the midst of a wheel." To the turnspits, "wheel" was a strong reminder of hard work, and "they all clapt their tails between their legs and ran out of the church."

For several centuries thereafter dogs were commonly used in the church as foot-warmers for the congregation. Special dog-minders were employed to keep them under control with "dog nawpers." In 1636 the Bishop of Norwich had special rails and pillars built to keep the dogs away from the Communion bread.

Go thou with this man, and God, which dwelleth in heaven, prosper your journey, and the angel of God keep you company. So they went forth, and the young man's dog with them.
—from *The Apocrypha: Tobit, v. 16*

Personal Thoughts About Animals

by C. S. Lewis

Can We Love Animals Too Much?

August 18, 1956

Dear Mary,

. . . I will never laugh at anyone for grieving over a loved beast. I think God wants us to love Him *more*, not to love creatures (even animals) *less*. We love everything in *one* way too much (i.e., at the expense of our love for Him) but in another way we love everything too little.

No person, animal, flower, or even pebble has ever been loved too much—i.e., more than every one of God's works deserves. But you need not feel "like a murderer" [to have euthanized a suffering pet]. Rather rejoice that God's law allows you to extend to Fanda that last mercy which (no doubt, quite rightly) we are forbidden to extend to suffering humans. You'll get over this . . . .

God bless you—and Fanda!

About Cats:

October 2, 1962

Dear Mary,

. . . I am glad to hear you have rehabilitated a displaced cat. I can't understand the people who say cats are not affectionate. Our Siamese (my "step-cat") is almost suffocatingly so. True, our ginger Tom (a great Don Juan and a mighty hunter before the Lord) will take no notice of *me*, but he will of others. He thinks I'm not quite socially up to his standards, and makes this very clear. No creature can give such a crushing "snub" as a cat! He sometimes looks at the dog—a big Boxer puppy, very anxious to be friendly—in a way that makes it want to sink to the floor . . . .

Will Animals Be Part of the Resurrection?

November 26, 1962

Dear Mary,

. . . My stuff about animals came long ago in *The Problem of*

*Pain.** I ventured the supposal—it could be nothing more—that as we are raised *in* Christ, so at least some animals are raised *in* us. Who knows, indeed, but that a great deal even of the inanimate creation is raised *in* the redeemed souls who have, during this life, taken its beauty into themselves? That may be the way the "new heaven and the new earth" are formed. Of course we can only guess and wonder. But these particular guesses arise in me, I trust, from taking seriously the resurrection of the body: a doctrine which now-a-days is very soft pedalled by nearly all the faithful—to our great impoverishment.

—from *Letters to an American Lady*

---

* Refers to Lewis's best-selling book *The Problem of Pain,* available from your local bookstore or from Macmillan Publishing Company, 100 K Brown Street, Riverside, NJ 08370.

A Counseling Psychologist Answers the Questions Families Ask Most About Pets

by Rebecca L. True

*R*ebecca True, R.N., M.A., M.F.C.C., *spent a number of years as a pediatric nurse, gaining extensive experience with critically and chronically ill children and grieving families. She now does marriage, family, and child counseling. With her husband, a psychiatrist, she has for several years practiced with a group of Christian counselors in Northern California.*

What are some of the psychological benefits pets can offer to families?

One of the best things animals can do is to help families learn about relationships. Starting very early, kids can begin to expand their awareness of the world beyond their own family through books and stories about pets. Later, as they gain experience with real-life pets, kids can learn valuable lessons about love, empathy, and even about loss and grief. Of course, they can also learn about sex and procreation by observing animals during pregnancy and when they give birth. Even if the family's own pets don't have babies, kids can be taken to zoos, kennels, farms, or to a neighbor's house to watch the birth process. These experiences are ideal opportunities for families to talk openly about reproduction.

Pets also are ideal examples for children. They give unconditional love—something we very rarely (if ever) experience in human relationships. It's easier for kids to understand the unconditional love of God if they can sample a bit of that kind of love from a dog or cat. Even parents who love their children very deeply tend to attach conditions to their love without realizing it. As a result, it's possible for a child to grow up without knowing what it's like to be loved exactly the way he is—even at his very worst—without being rejected, betrayed, belittled, or shamed for "falling short." Dogs and cats are especially good at giving children that kind of experience. Kids quickly learn that they can tell their pets the secret thoughts that no one else can be trusted with. Animals are there to comfort and to share the important moments in life. Friends may walk away in the middle of a crisis, but the dog or cat will stay by your side as long as it's needed. A pet neither lectures nor admonishes; it simply listens, responds, and comforts in a thoroughly satisfying way.

Animals also can teach lessons about life in the real world. For example, when you're trying to explain to a child the difference between "safe" and "unsafe" people—those who can and can't be trusted—the child will understand much more easily if you explain in terms of animals. You can say, "We trust our own dog because we know her so well. We know what she'll do if we pet her and play with her. But we never approach or try to touch a dog we don't know, because that dog might bite. It might seem friendly, but until we've known that dog for a long time we don't trust it to come near enough to hurt us." This kind of example often brings home a vital message that would otherwise not get through. These lessons carry through to the child's relationships with people, too.

Children today spend much more time alone than they did in the days when most moms stayed at home to take care of them. Now, the family home can be a lonely, frightening place for "latchkey" kids who let themselves into an empty house to wait for parents, brothers or sisters to get home. Pets can make "goin' home time" a much happier prospect for these youngsters. A friendly wag or a warm purr can say "welcome home" in just the way a child needs to hear it. Pets are also good for kids experiencing other kinds of loneliness—divorce, a new baby brother or sister, or a death in the family, for example. In times like that, it's reassuring to have a loving relationship that's predictable and unchanging.

How can parents know when their children are ready for a pet, and how can they choose a pet that will be ideal for their family?

First, I think it's important to avoid impulsive pet ownership. It's amazing how many people get a pet simply because their kids bring one home, or they see a cute puppy or kitten in a shop window and buy it on the spur of the moment. Parents who want to avoid problems should never get a family pet without preparing for it over time.

It's always wise to have a "waiting period" before bringing a pet into the family. No matter how children may beg, cry, pout, or plead, it's important to be sure the child is really ready for the reponsibilities a pet will involve. Every child will promise to take care of the new pet, but remember, kids aren't born understanding what it means to have an animal's life and welfare depend on them.

During the waiting period—which should be at least a month, but ideally would be much longer—the family can talk together about what sort of pet would be happiest in their household. Some questions they could discuss might be:

— What do we expect a pet to do for us—individually and as a family? Children should talk about why they want the particular pet they have in mind. Parents can gain new insights into the needs of their children and steer them toward appropriate pets.

— How will a pet fit into the framework of our daily life?

— What activities are we involved in that can include the pet?

— Will we want the pet in the house most of the time, or outside? Dogs especially need large doses of human companionship to be happy. Nothing is more miserable than an "outside dog" who spends his days longing for the company of owners whose lives are too busy to devote a few hours a day to him. Active families that can't spend time with a dog should opt for a cat, a bird, or another more independent creature that won't suffer as much from loneliness.

— How much time will each of us realistically want to spend feeding, training, grooming, and playing with a pet? If this will be a family pet (as opposed to little Jennifer's or Bobby's pet), parents need to decide how much responsibility they're willing to take, and spell that out in clearly defined terms. It's a good idea to list all the "chores" that will have to be done once the pet is a part of the household, and divide them up among the family members based on which jobs each person is willing to commit to on a permanent basis. If parents discover that nobody wants to do the more onerous chores like cleaning the birdcage or the litter box, they'll have a clue about how things will go when the pet actually arrives. It's up to the parents to set limits on how responsibility should be shared.

— How much money can we afford to spend on a pet? How much per month can we allocate for food, veterinary care, boarding while we're away, and other regular expenses? Children can visit grocery stores with parents to check the prices of food various pets might need, and then talk about what it costs for licenses, annual shots, emergencies, and other ordinary expenses. This can be an opportunity for parents to teach practical lessons about planning, budgeting, and taking responsibility for our actions.

— Is the size and energy level of the pet we're considering appropriate for our family? Is it too big (or too small) for the children to handle easily? Is it safe? Could this animal harm a child? It's remarkable how many families blindly chose a "macho" dog—a Doberman or a pit bull, for example—without consideration for the safety and peace of mind of the children in the home. Children can be terrorized when they're forced to live with animals that threaten them or play too rough. Aggressive dogs usually come from a long line of "working dogs," and they don't belong with children who can't control them.

— What will happen if the pet we're considering doesn't meet our needs as well as we had hoped? Family members should talk about how they will deal with this possibility. Again, planning can help avoid problems.

You know the old, familiar story: Mom and Dad get a cat or dog for Junior because he promises a thousand times that he'll feed it, walk it, groom it, and take it everywhere. Mom and Dad, suckers that they are, tell themselves a pet might be a good idea because it will teach Junior to be responsible. Usually in about a month Junior begins to "forget" the feeding and walking, and soon Mom, Dad and Junior are bickering constantly about the responsibilities Junior seems to be shirking. Saddest of all, the pet becomes a burden instead of a cherished member of the family. How can parents keep this sort of thing from happening?

It's a bad idea to get a pet "to teach responsibility." It almost always boomerangs. What actually happens is that kids learn to *resent* and *avoid* responsibility—and that's a terrible lesson that ends up hurting kids, parents, *and* pets.

This relates to the "waiting period" I talked about before. Parents have to evaluate how much responsibility each child is actually able to take for a pet based on factors like age, past experience, maturity, and a realistic appraisal of the child's motivation.

Don't get a pet that will be a burden to your children—or to you, if you end up having to take care of it. Regardless of how much whining and begging your kids do, firmly refuse to give in to their desire for a pet until you're positive they can *easily* handle the responsibility, and have shown it through progressively more and more responsible actions in other areas of their lives. A child who has never taken responsibility for cleaning up his room or fixing a simple meal, for example, is not ready for the much larger responsibilities of pet ownership. Let him practice on progressively more and more responsible tasks before you allow him to enter into a relationship with a pet.

As parents, we have to balance what's possible and reasonable to expect from our children with the child's true motivations. During your "waiting period" you'll have the time to see what the child really wants from a pet, and you can then decide whether it's merely a passing phase or something more enduring. If your child says, "everyone has a dog" or complains that "my friend Jennifer has a kitten, so I should have one, too," you'll know that her real motivation is simply to own something everyone else owns—like a new pair of shoes or a T-shirt. When the fad wears off, the pet will be tossed aside just the way the shoes and T-shirt are when they're no longer new and exciting. Instead of giving in, you can simply wait for the desire to pass.

Look for signs that the child is interested in a long-term *relationship* with the pet. After all, a family pet's biggest function in our lives is to fulfill our needs—both emotionally and spiritually. If it doesn't do that, it becomes nothing more than a nuisance in our lives. That's sad—both for the pet and its owners. How does your child do in relationships with friends? Do you see compassion, empathy, and the desire to anticipate and meet others' needs in your child's behavior—or do you see selfishness and a lack of interest in others? Don't expect that your child will magically transform into a compassionate, caring person if he isn't that way *before* you get a pet. Look for evidence that the child wants more than just another toy.

Another problem that seems to come up in the area of responsibility is the matter of what happens when a pet simply doesn't work out. Parents too often force the issue, demanding that their children take responsibility for the fate of the animal when they may be incapable of doing so. A good rule is that children should never be forced to be parents. And asking a young child to decide

the fate of a pet is doing just that. It teaches even *more* resentment of responsibility instead of helping the child grow. Parents have to deal with reality. Before a pet is brought home, parents should decide what they'll do if their child isn't able to handle the pet—in spite of their best efforts to assure success. They should develop a contingency plan, because that's realistic. A child doesn't learn anything good when his parents simply dispose of a pet like a broken toy and then tell him it's his fault.

How can we help a child—or another adult, for that matter—deal with the death of a pet?

One of the sad facts about relationships with animals is that we can expect to lose them long before we would lose a human companion to death. Even a very long-lived dog or cat will not normally live beyond fifteen or sixteen years. Some larger dogs live much shorter lives. It may help ease the pain of a pet's death if it grows old with the family. There can be a gradual winding down of the relationship as the animal grows older; the family can take time to get used to the idea that this pet will not live much longer. They can prepare for the separation together. If you have the chance to prepare, you can begin to grieve before the fact. But when pets die in accidents or simply disappear from our lives, or when they die from heart attacks or unexpected illnesses, the grieving process is complicated by shock.

It seems to be hardest of all when we must make the decision to put a pet to sleep because it's in pain or has an irreversible disease. Children need help dealing with the sometimes overwhelming feelings of loss, guilt, sadness, and fear that are generated when we must make that choice.

It's a mistake to tell children (or adults, for that matter) not to feel sad, not to cry, or not to think about the loss of a pet. Never dismiss the death of a beloved animal by saying "it was *only* a dog (or cat, gerbil, or bird)." That attitude demeans and devalues the positive feelings and genuine love that were experienced in a very real and important relationship. The loss of a pet will mean that those who loved the pet will mourn, and that mourning should be permitted and respected in the family. It isn't very different from the mourning that takes place when we lose the people we love.

The death of a pet can be an opportunity for families to talk about loss and sadness. Parents can talk about the pets they've lost in the past and how they handled their grief. The family can cry together and allow each other to grieve individually, sympathizing and comforting each other in special ways. People don't usually get much understanding or help from outside the family when a pet dies. If I said to someone, "My mother died," I'd get great sympathy, but if I said, "My cat died," I'd get very little. Most people would say, "Too bad," and let it go at that. But the depth of our grief over the loss of a pet can be just as signficant as in the loss of a member of the family, depending on the closeness of the human or animal relationship. We need to experience that grief, not stifle it.

Sometimes it helps a family to have a funeral for a pet. It's a means of saying final farewells. It acknowledges that death has taken place and the relationship is over. In my own childhood we had an elaborate funeral when our dog died. We sang hymns, gathered flowers, and made a wreath for the service we held at the grave, which was in a field near the house. Over the years that followed, we visited the grave with fresh flowers and remembered the good years we had together. Some friends of ours had a pet cemetery for all the pets that died in their family. I thought it was a good idea—it gave appropriate dignity and importance to the animals that had enriched their lives.

Another thing that can be helpful is simply to reminisce about the pet and the things that were unique about it. As a family you can visit the places your pet played, look at photographs, and even put mementoes like a collar, a food dish, or a favorite toy in a special place of honor. All of this will enable the family to further the process of grieving which will finally allow everyone to move forward.

The mourning process with pets can last anywhere from a few days to many months, just as it can with people. It's quite individual. I remember a little boy I counseled whose cat died. He cried and grieved over the loss of the cat far more deeply than he did over the really enormous problems he was facing in his family. Actually, the rule about grieving is that it's different for everyone, and we have to allow for those differences and let people do what they must to get through it.

Parents naturally worry if children seem to be carrying their sadness too long, but I think they should be more concerned when their children don't seem to grieve at all. Occasionally grief can become exaggerated and unhealthy, and that's usually pretty obvious—the loss crowds out everything else in life for many months or perhaps years. In those rare cases professional counseling might be helpful. But most of the time the healthiest thing

is for the grieving person to work through the pain with the
support of those who understand and permit the process to be
thoroughly accomplished. That's what family members should be
able to do.

Gradually, depending on the length and intensity of the relationships between people and pet, recovery begins. Thoughts
about the animal become less frequent and we begin to shift from
thoughts of death toward thoughts of life. We find that we can
talk about the pet and it hurts less than it did a month ago. We're
able to remember the good times without crying. There may be
moments when grief unexpectedly wells up again, and that may
go on for years but eventually—in our own time—we heal.

Is it a good idea to try to bring a new pet into the family as soon as possible to help ease the feelings of loss?

Not always, but it really depends on the family. Some need to
wait until the pain of the loss has completely healed. Others may
not need extended periods of mourning. As important as grief
can be, it's just as important not to force anyone to grieve, or to
make him feel guilty for not being sad for a long time. Sometimes
a child will begin to recover from a loss by *asking* for a new pet. In
those cases, there's nothing wrong with talking it over as a family
and deciding it's time for another animal. But remember, we can
never truly *replace* any pet. Each one has a unique spot in our
hearts, and it's unfair to expect a new animal to take the place of
one that dies.

Hoping to distract a child from his grief, many parents quickly
bring in a new pet they expect to erase all the painful memories of
the one that's died. Unfortunately, this doesn't usually spare the
child any pain. What it really does is deny him the privilege of
mourning. It's often wisest to take a few months out for grieving
the loss of one pet before bringing another on the scene. Rushing
into a new dog or cat may suggest to a child that those we love are
easily disposed of and replaced. Sometimes a child will have
secret fears that because his parents seemed to feel no pain over
the loss of a pet and quickly "replaced" it with another, they
might be capable of doing the same thing with him. Children
need to be reassured that the people and animals they love are
irreplaceable, and are never forgotten. They also need to learn
from experience that the pain of loss eventually gets better, and
we go on with life. It's through such experiences that children can
gain the courage to open themselves to loving relationships with

new animals (and people) in spite of the fact that they may one day part.

My husband and I had a golden retriever named Taffy who was stolen when she was a year and a half old. I had grown terribly attached to her, and it was very hard for me to get over that loss. I was so upset, in fact, that I made up my mind never to get attached to an animal again. But eventually I finished grieving and realized that the process had stretched me as a person. I made a decision not to remain detached, not to ignore and shut out the animals that could be a wonderful, joyous part of my life. I wanted the fun and pleasure that animals could bring, so eventually I chose to take the risk that comes with attachment. That's an important step for all of us. With animals as with people, love carries with it the possibility of loss and pain. But if we don't accept that possibility, we miss a lot of love and our lives are poorer for it.

How do you answer children when they ask if their pet has gone to heaven?

I avoid dogmatic responses. Parents often mistake a child's questions about where the dead animal has gone as a request for theological answers. That's almost never the case. Kids don't think in those terms. Actually, they're looking for two distinct things: First, to have their emotions satisfied, and second, to get a clear, satisfying visual picture of where the pet is now.

Children often have scary, unsettling fears about death which lead them to picture their pets (and people, too) trapped under the cold, damp earth without anyone to take care of them. Parents can help children satisfy the emotional need for reassurance by explaining that the pet is not "down there"—that it has left behind its skin and bones and has gone to a place where it's safe and warm, where it can be taken care of and loved just as well as it was by the child.

To help a child get the visual picture that will comfort him best, parents can ask the child, "What kind of place do you think God would create for the pet you and He loved so much?" Allow the child to fantasize about the perfect eternal home for the pet. Parents are often delighted and surprised by the elaborate, colorful fantasies their children have about what heaven should be like for a pet. If a child says, "I think Tinkerbell is somewhere in outer space playing in a big glass house full of catnip and Meow Mix," a parent can say, "I'd like to think that, too. That sounds like just the kind of thing God might have in store for her." This sort of discussion can be enormously comforting, both for the child and for the parent. When the parent avoids getting caught up in theological answers the child can't comprehend anyway, a real opportunity for communication occurs. And the child begins to understand God in terms he or she *can* relate to—visual pictures representing safety, love, comfort, and joy.

Through this whole process, parents will find many chances to insure that kids learn positive lessons about relationships, loss, God, and love. Above all, when families face the loss of a treasured animal, they need to reassure one another that God loves animals *and* people, and that He will provide whatever is best and most perfect for each of us.

A re not two sparrows sold for a farthing? and one of them shall not fall to the ground without your Father.

—Matthew 10:29

Pet Population

There are an estimated 58 million cats living in U.S. homes. Also, 52 million dogs, 45 million birds, 260 million fish (give or take a guppy), and another 125 million other creatures are kept as pets.

Dogs rush in where cats fear to tread.

—Anonymous

Pet Prints

Award-winning artist Pat McLaughlin, whose charming drawings of cats and dogs appear in this book, makes her work available to the public in the form of signed and numbered limited-edition prints and on note cards and stationery. Most of her depictions of pets are taken from real-life animals whose owners supply her with photos. Owners whose pets become McLaughlin originals are given the first signed print in the series. Write for her catalog: Art Studio Workshops, 518 Schilling Circle, N.W., Forest Lake, Minnesota 55025; (612) 464-5623.

Pets for People

Thousands of senior citizens around the country are now being matched with dogs and cats through a new pet adoption program offered by Ralston Purina Company and local humane societies and SPCAs. The Pets for People Program unites people sixty years of age or older with homeless shelter pets completely free of charge.

More than ninety animal shelters in seventy cities are offering the program. Purina donates a hundred dollars to the shelter for each pet adopted by a senior citizen. The donation covers the adoption fee and a complete health checkup by a veterinarian (including inoculations and spaying or neutering) for each pet. Prospective pet owners are carefully screened to be sure the animals will get plenty of love and affection and that their practical needs will be met. Each newly adopted pet comes with a free starter supply of dog or cat food, a new leash, food and water bowls, and a booklet on how to take care of the pet. In return, owners attend an orientation session to learn the responsibilities of caring for a pet and agree to give the pet a good home. Later, the program staff check with owners to be sure they're getting along well and that the animals are in good hands.

Most program participants choose cats and dogs that are at least a year old. Adult pets are ideal for older people because they're usually trained and housebroken. Their manners are generally better than those of puppies and kittens, and they don't need as much care.

The matches that have been made in the first year of the program have proven beneficial to both the pets and their new owners. Many owners have discovered that their new furry friends are better for their health than any tonic or medicine they've tried. A number of studies have shown that pets can be instrumental in speeding recovery from illness, lowering blood pressure, and curing depression—a common problem among older people. Pets reduce feelings of isolation and loneliness which can plague those who retire from an active life or are suddenly living alone after many years of marriage. Pets even increase their owners' resistance to disease by providing a source of love, comfort, and security. Research has shown that the quality of life can dramatically improve when an older person has a pet to look after.

Participants in the Pets for People Program agree. A survey of those who first adopted pets showed that nearly 100 percent said their pet was a good friend or companion, 97 percent felt happier since they had gotten the pet, and 93 percent felt less lonely. And the vast majority said they felt healthier and that their pet gave them an added incentive to exercise.

With more than 8 million elderly Americans living alone and many more millions of unwanted animals in animal shelters, the time seems right for these two groups to get together in a mutually rewarding way.

For applications or information, call your local shelter or write the Purina Pets for People Program, Checkerboard Square, St. Louis, Missouri 63164.

The Ten Commandments of Pet Ownership

by Dr. Michael W. Fox

Pets give people lots of pleasure. In return, people should treat pets right. If you're a pet owner, commit yourself to these 10 basic rules:

1. *Treat all companion animals humanely—with patience, compassion, understanding and consideration for their needs.*

   Humane treatment is what we owe pets in return for their wonderful companionship and unconditional affection. Being humane to all creatures also helps us become better people.

2. *Promise to uphold your pet's basic rights.*

   Bringing a new animal home is like taking in a new child. Before you decide to have a pet, be sure you can give it the time, attention and proper care it's entitled to.

   All animals have the right to a clean and quiet place to sleep. No pets should be allowed to roam free and unsupervised.

3. *Give your pets fresh water and a complete and balanced diet daily.*

   Clean your pet's water bowl and fill with fresh water every day. Likewise, always give it a variety of food that's fresh, not stale. Buy foods that offer a complete and balanced diet.

4. *Know the needs of your pet and fulfill them as best as you possibly can.*

   Read about the type of pet you have and about its particular needs. Most animals require regular exercise, playtime, companionship, and grooming. Most also enjoy the company of their own kind.

5. *Give your pet regular veterinary care.*

   All pets are likely to get sick at some time. You should be prepared to pay for veterinary treatment. Read up on the signs of illness your pet can show. These can include disinterest in food or water and being less playful and less responsive to you. Frequent sneezing, difficult breathing, a discharge from the nose or eyes, diarrhea, and displays of aggressive behavior when touched signal that your pet needs to go to the animal doctor.

6. *It's wrong for people to take an animal from the wild and keep it for a pet.*

   Wild animals belong in the wild, not in captivity. Keeping a raccoon or fox in a small cage, for example, is cruel and inhumane.

   Raising an orphaned baby rabbit or bird until it's old enough to be released back into the wild is fine. But resist the temptation to try to make such wildlife into pets.

7. *Watch your animal and learn to understand its behavior.*

   Being very attentive and interpreting your animal's behavior carefully will help you avoid punishing it unfairly. Some examples: it's natural for puppies to chew things up, because they are teething. Cats and dogs sometimes become unhousebroken because of an infection or because they are upset by the presence of a new pet or baby in the home. Animals often bite when they are afraid or in pain. Don't punish pets for any of these behaviors. If necessary, take them to a vet, who can determine what the problem is.

8. *Give your pet obedience training.*

   Your dog should be raised so it won't bother other people and so it will be easy to handle. Always keep your dog on a leash outdoors and train it to obey such simple commands as "sit," "stay," and "come." And *never* strike an animal. A firm and sharp command is enough.

9. *When euthanasia is required, make sure the animal dies painlessly and with dignity.*

   "Euthanasia" means humane death. Ten to 13 million unwanted cats and dogs are euthanized in animal shelters each year—because irresponsible owners fail to have their pets neutered to prevent breeding.

   But there are times when euthanasia is the best choice: when an animal is so old, sick or injured that its health cannot be restored. It's far better to end, rather than prolong, incurable suffering.

10. *Everyone who cares about animals should defend any animal being treated inhu-*

manely. And they should share with others these 10 Commandments of Pet Ownership.

Whenever you see someone mistreating an animal immediately report it to your local animal control authority or the police. Animals are our companions, so we should be their protectors. I call this *humane stewardship.* For all the many ways they enrich our lives, it's the least we can do.

Dr. Michael W. Fox is the Scientific Director of the Humane Society of the United States.

Want to Help Animals?

The *Animal Activist's Handbook,* available from the Animal Protection Institute (P.O. Box 22505, Sacramento, California 95822) will tell you everything you need to know to get started. This comprehensive, beautifully illustrated guide (complete with numerous case histories) tells you how to go about making the world a safer, sounder place for animals regardless of where you live. 103 pages, $2.75.

Also available from the Institute:

- Bookmarks: "Purr-fect Care of Cats" (Dog and Bird bookmarks also available). Lists responsibilities of animal ownership. Great for kids. 100 for $2.00.
- Colorful stamps featuring art from API's children's art contests.
- Bumper stickers: "Stand Up For Animals"; "Be an Animal's Best Friend." $1.00.
- Window decal for house or car: "Animals Inside." 50 cents each.
- T-shirts: "Stand Up For Animals." S-M-L, Children's size, $8.00. Adult S-M-L-XL, $10.00 (for men or women).
- Finding Good Homes for Pets: Brochure. Free.
- How to Become Involved for Animals in Your Community: Brochure. Free.
- Children's Reading List. 35 cents.
- Cat Care, Dog Care brochures: 15 cents.
- Posters: Large, beautiful and colorful—a natural for kids' rooms and offices.

The Pettable Kingdom Mystery Poster	$2.00
How to Care for Your Pet	$2.00
Wildlife Under Attack	$3.00

- Sun Shields for cars: Accordion-fold, heavy-duty shields to place inside your front window. One side asks for help in an emergency, the other says "Don't Park Your Pet" and explains the problems of heat stroke when animals are left inside cars on warm days.

Dead Collie

I'll not catch such a flurry of living and grace.
   To chase down the wind is sheer folly:
Just say that my life has a void lifeless place
   For a little dead collie.

Still I muse on your goodness—so glad to be good—
   Free courtesy ruled your brief living,
Never thinking you could disobey if you would,
   And purely forgiving.

A whistle from me and you whirled from your play,
   Up ears and eager paws drumming,
Your duty and wishes all one in the gay
   Swift rush of your coming.

Even now a clear whistle might reach and surpass
   All limits and bring back the rushing
Of printless gay paws running over the grass,
   And the silky head brushing.

     —from *A Severe Mercy* by Sheldon Vanauken

A really companiable and indispensable dog is an accident
of nature. You can't get it by breeding for it, and you can't
buy it with money. It just happens along.

E. B. White

Memoirs of a Yellow Dog

by O. Henry

I don't suppose it will knock any of you people off your perch to read a contribution from an animal. Mr. Kipling and a good many others have demonstrated the fact that animals can express themselves in remunerative English, and no magazine goes to press nowadays without an animal story in it, except the old-style monthlies that are still running pictures of Bryan and the Mont Pelée horror.

But you needn't look for any stuck-up literature in my piece, such as Bearoo, the bear, and Snakoo, the snake, and Tammanoo, the tiger, talk in the jungle books. A yellow dog that's spent most of his life in a cheap New York flat, sleeping in a corner on an old sateen underskirt (the one she spilled port wine on at the Lady Longshoremen's banquet), mustn't be expected to perform any tricks with the art of speech.

I was born a yellow pup; date, locality, pedigree, and weight unknown. The first thing I can recollect, an old woman had me in a basket at Broadway and Twenty-third trying to sell me to a fat lady. Old Mother Hubbard was boosting me to beat the band as a genuine Pomeranian-Hambletonian - Red - Irish - Cochin - China - Stoke-Pogis fox terrier. The fat lady chased a *V* around among the samples of grosgrain flannelette in her shopping bag till she cornered it, and gave up. From that moment on I was a pet—a mamma's own wootsey squidlums. Say, gentle reader, did you ever have a two-hundred-pound woman breathing a flavor of Camembert cheese and Peau d'Espagne pick you up and wallop her nose all over you, remarking all the time in an Emma Eames tone of voice: "Oh, oo's um oodlum, doodlum, woodlum, toodlum, bitsy-witsy skoodlums"?

From a pedigreed yellow pup I grew up to be an anonymous yellow cur looking like a cross between an Angora cat and a box of lemons. But my mistress never tumbled. She thought that the two primeval pups that Noah chased into the ark were but a collateral branch of my ancestors. It took two policemen to keep her from entering me at the Madison Square Garden for the Siberian bloodhound prize.

I'll tell you about that flat. The house was the ordinary thing in New York, paved with Parian marble in the entrance hall and cobblestones above the first floor. Our flat was three fl—well, not flights—climbs up. My mistress rented it unfurnished, and put in the regular things—1903 antique upholstered parlor set, oil chromo of geishas in a Harlem teahouse, rubber plant, and husband.

By Sirius! There was a biped I felt sorry for. He was a little man with sandy hair and whiskers a good deal like mine. Henpecked? Well, toucans and flamingos and pelicans all had their bills in him. He wiped the dishes and listened to my mistress tell about the cheap, ragged things the lady with the squirrel-skin coat on the second floor hung out on her line to dry. And every evening while she was getting supper she made him take me out on the end of a string for a walk.

If men knew how women pass the time when they are alone they'd never marry. Laura Jean Libbey, peanut brittle, a little almond cream on the neck muscles, dishes unwashed, half an hour's talk with the iceman, reading a package of old letters, a couple of pickles and two bottles of malt extract, one hour peeking through a hole in the window shade into the flat across the air shaft—that's about all there is to it. Twenty minutes before time for him to come home from work she straightens up the house, fixes her rat so it won't show, and gets out a lot of sewing for a ten-minute bluff.

I led a dog's life in that flat. 'Most all day I lay there in my corner watching that fat woman kill time. I slept sometimes and had pipe dreams about being out chasing cats into basements and growling at old ladies with black mittens, as a dog was intended to do. Then she would pounce upon me with a lot of that driveling poodle palaver and kiss me on the nose—but what could I do? A dog can't chew cloves.

I began to feel sorry for Hubby, dog my cats if I didn't. We looked so much alike that people noticed it when we went out; so we shook the streets that Morgan's cab drives down, and took to climbing the piles of last December's snow on the streets where cheap people live.

One evening when we were thus promenading, and I was trying to look like a prize Saint Bernard, and the old man was trying to look like he wouldn't have murdered the first organ-grinder he heard play Mendelssohn's wedding march, I looked up at him and said, in my way:

"What are you looking so sour about, you oakum-trimmed

lobster? She don't kiss you. You don't have to sit on her lap and listen to talk that would make the book of a musical comedy sound like the maxims of Epictetus. You ought to be thankful you're not a dog. Brace up, Benedick, and bid the blues begone."

The matrimonial mishap looked down at me with almost canine intelligence on his face.

"Why, doggie," says he, "good doggie. You almost look like you could speak. What is it, doggie—cats?"

Cats! Could speak!

But, of course, he couldn't understand. Humans were denied the speech of animals. The only common ground of communication upon which dogs and men can get together is in fiction.

In the flat across the hall from us lived a lady with a black-and-tan terrier. Her husband strung it and took it out every evening, but he always came home cheerful and whistling. One day I touched noses with the black-and-tan in the hall, and I struck him for an elucidation.

"See here, Wiggle-and-Skip," I says, "you know that it ain't the nature of a real man to play dry nurse to a dog in public. I never saw one leashed to a bowwow yet that didn't look like he'd like to lick every other man that looked at him. But your boss comes in every day as perky and set up as an amateur prestidigitator doing the egg trick. How does he do it? Don't tell me he likes it."

"Him?" says the black-and-tan. "Why, he uses Nature's Own Remedy. He gets spifflicated. At first when we go out he's as shy as the man on the steamer who would rather play pedro when they make 'em all jackpots. By the time we've been in eight saloons he don't care whether the thing on the end of his line is a dog or a catfish. I've lost two inches of my tail trying to sidestep those swinging doors."

The pointer I got from that terrier—vaudeville, please copy—set me to thinking.

One evening about six o'clock my mistress ordered him to get busy and do the ozone act for Lovey. I have concealed it until now, but that is what she called me. The black-and-tan was called "Tweetness." I consider that I have the bulge on him as far as you could chase a rabbit. Still, "Lovely" is something of a nomenclatural tin can on the tail of one's self-respect.

At a quiet place on a safe street I tightened the line of my custodian in front of an attractive, refined saloon. I made a dead-ahead scramble for the doors, whining like a dog in the press dispatches that lets the family know that little Alice is bogged while gathering lilies in the brook.

"Why, darn my eyes," says the old man, with a grin, "darn my eyes if the saffron-colored son of a seltzer lemonade ain't asking me in to take a drink. Lemme see—how long's it been since I saved shoe leather by keeping one foot on the footrest? I believe I'll—"

I knew I had him. Hot Scotches he took, sitting at a table. For an hour he kept the Campbells coming. I sat by his side rapping for the waiter with my tail, and eating free lunch such as mamma in her flat never equaled with her homemade truck bought at a delicatessen store eight minutes before papa comes home.

When the products of Scotland were all exhausted except the rye bread the old man unwound me from the table leg and played me outside like a fisherman plays a salmon. Out there he took off my collar and threw it into the street.

"Poor doggie," says he, "good doggie. She shan't kiss you any more. 'Sa darned shame. Good doggie, go away and get run over by a streetcar and be happy."

I refused to leave. I leaped and frisked around the old man's legs happy as a pug on a rug.

"You old flea-headed woodchuck-chaser," I said to him, "you moon-baying, rabbit-pointing, egg-stealing old beagle, can't you see that I don't want to leave you? Can't you see that we're both Pups in the Wood and the missus is the cruel uncle after you with the dish towel and me with the flea liniment and a pink bow to tie on my tail. Why not cut that all out and be pards forever more?"

Maybe you'll say he didn't understand—maybe he didn't. But he kind of got a grip on the Hot Scotches, and stood still for a minute, thinking.

"Doggie," says he, finally, "we don't live more than a dozen lives on this earth, and very few of us live to be more than three hundred. If I ever see that flat any more I'm a flat, and if you do you're flatter; and that's no flattery. I'm offering sixty to one that Westward Ho wins out by the length of a dachshund."

There was no string, but I frolicked along with my master to the Twenty-third Street ferry. And the cats on the route saw reason to give thanks that prehensile claws had been given them.

On the Jersey side my master said to a stranger who stood eating a currant bun:

"Me and my doggie, we are bound for the Rocky Mountains."

But what pleased me most was when my old man pulled both of my ears until I howled, and said:

"You common, monkey-headed, rat-tailed, sulphur-colored son of a doormat, do you know what I'm going to call you?"

I thought of "Lovey," and I whined dolefully.

"I'm going to call you 'Pete,' " says my master; and if I'd had five tails I couldn't have done enough wagging to do justice to the occasion.

How Children See Their Pets

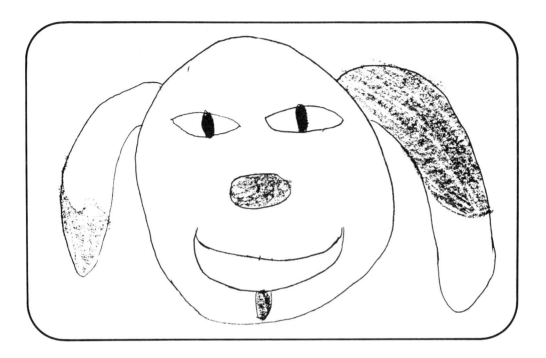

Dogs as Marriage Counselors?

Recent research at a major midwestern university suggests that dogs may be good for what ails a marriage. Couples were invited to talk about and try to resolve conflicts in their relationships in sessions with and without their pet dogs in attendance. When dogs were present—whether the couple was happily or unhappily married—the climate for conflict resolution was enhanced. The dog's presence seemed to have something of a soothing effect on physical responses that were measured during conflict, and this helped both happily and unhappily married couples deal with their problems more effectively.

Canine Court

Los Angeles city officials finally had enough. With 1,200 to 1,700 animal nuisance complaints to handle every year—about 10 percent of which ended in lawsuits in the city's already over-dogged court system—the city attorney's office decided to create a "canine court" to arbitrate disputes, save money, and give the judges a break. Each trial was costing the city around $3,500 a day.

A prominent dog trainer has volunteered to be the hearings officer. Claiming he speaks "dog-ese," the trainer tries to help animals and owners work out their differences outside the courtroom. He often demonstrates to owners how to keep their dogs from barking and shows them ways of breaking the animals of destructive, nuisance-type behavior. Not content to let sleeping dogs lie, he keeps in personal contact with the parties in each dispute to be sure the complaint has been resolved to everyone's satisfaction.

Test Your Pet I.Q.

by Francis Sheridan Goulart

A well-informed pet owner provides the best TLC for his cat or dog. How much of what you know about your cat or dog is on target? Test it out. The following information is provided by the Pets Are Wonderful Council (PAW), the American Kennel Society, the American Humane Society, and the American Feline Society.

True or False?

1. No one has ever died from a dog bite.
   Answer: False. Dogs put the bite on one million of us a year, the *American Medical Journal* says, and although it's rare, a dog's bite *can* be fatal.
2. Cat lovers spend $2 billion a year on cat food.
   Answer: True.
3. The average dog is as smart as a three- to four-year-old child.
   Answer: True.
4. Hamburger is a good food for adult dogs.
   Answer: False—too much fat.
5. It costs $300 to take care of a medium-size dog for one year.
   Answer: False. It's closer to $400, the Humane Society says.
6. A neutered cat gets fat, and there's nothing you can do.
   Answer: False. Neutering changes the metabolism, but exercise and proper feeding will prevent obesity.
7. The gentlest of the big dogs and the one least likely to bite is the Labrador retriever.
   Answer: True.
8. A high-fish diet every day is not good for cats.
   Answer: True. It can cause yellow fat disease.
9. You can't teach an old dog new tricks.
   Answer: False. Older dogs actually learn faster.
10. Every U.S. president has owned a cat or a dog.
    Answer: False. The six presidents who never owned anything

finny, feathered, or furry were John Adams, James K. Polk, Millard Fillmore, Franklin Pierce, James Buchanan, and Chester Arthur, the Dog Museum of America says.

11. Chocolate and milk give puppies worms.
    Answer: False. Milk's fine, but chocolate can make a puppy sick.
12. You can catch a cold from your cat.
    Answer: False. But cats can transmit streptococcus bacilli, as well as lice, rabies, and pinworms.
13. Dogs obey men better than they obey women.
    Answer: True. Dogs respond to a deeper tone of voice, but when a woman has an authoritative tone, a dog does just as well.
14. The dog name "Fido" means "faithful."
    Answer: True.
15. The most popular name for the bulldog in the U.S. is Spot.
    Answer: False. It's Winston.
16. Pets should be kept warmer than people.
    Answer: False. An overly warm house can disturb a cat's or dog's thermostat and cause hypothermia.
17. A small dog is easier to train than a large one.
    Answer: False. Size is not a major factor in training a dog.
18. Canine distemper is no longer a problem in the U.S.
    Answer: False. There are still enough cases to warrant vaccinations.
19. Cats never need people.
    Answer: False. They can become just as attached to their owners as can dogs.
20. Dogs see everything in black and white.
    Answer: True.
21. Unspayed female dogs often die of cancer.
    Answer: True.
22. Dogs and cats are natural enemies.
    Answer: False. Dogs and cats can live together harmoniously.
23. Purebreds are smarter than mixed breeds.
    Answer: False. There is no difference.
24. There are more pet dogs than cats in the U.S.
    Answer: False. For the first time, cats are in the majority.
25. The four most popular "color" names for dogs are Blackie, Midnight, Yellow, and Rusty.
    Answer: True.
26. When a cat rubs against you he's expressing affection.
    Answer: False. He's making you a part of his territory by rubbing his scent on you.

27. Shaving a dog's coat in summer will keep him cool.
    Answer: False. A dog's coat insulates him against both heat and cold. The coat protects him from sunburn and insects, including mosquitoes, which can carry heart-worms.
28. The normal dog needs only one or two baths a year.
    Answer: True. Frequent baths wash vitamins and natural oils from the coat.
29. Cats came to America with the Pilgrims in the 1600s.
    Answer: True.
30. Dogs don't like living in apartments.
    Answer: False. Dogs are happy as long as they get food, discipline, exercise, and TLC.
31. A dog or puppy best loves the person who feeds him.
    Answer: True.
32. Feline Leukemia, a cancer in cats, can now be prevented by vaccination.
    Answer: True.
33. All pets need lots of exercise.
    Answer: False. Only dogs bred for hunting and herding have high exercise requirements. And cats thrive on moderate activity.
34. A dog should be trained by only one member of the family.
    Answer: False. Every member of the family should help.
35. Cats are the only clawed animals that walk on their claws.
    Answer: True.
36. The Pekingese was regarded as sacred by Oriental royalty.
    Answer: True.
37. Once a dog has had guard-dog training, he can't be untrained.
    Answer: True.
38. Cats don't have a sweet tooth, but dogs do.
    Answer: True.
39. Guard dogs make the best protectors of the home.
    Answer: False. A guard dog is dangerous, even to the owner.

Scoring:
39–30: Excellent. You're a bow-*wow*.
29–18: Not bad.
17 or less: Time to bone up.

THE DOG'S MAJOR FACIAL EXPRESSIONS

Relaxed and confident

Ears back

Worried

Wrinkled brow

Suspicious   Lowered ears

Threat stare

Lips pulled back

Somewhat fearful

Fangs bared

Extremely fearful and threatening to bite

Apologetic

From HOW TO TALK TO YOUR ANIMALS, copyright © 1985 by Jean Craighead George.
Reproduced by permission of Harcourt Brace Jovanovich, Inc.

THE DOG'S TAIL POSITIONS

"Who's boss?"   "I'm boss."   "I'm somebody important."

"I'm depressed."   "I'm a terrible dog."   "I'm an omega."

"I'm about to fight."   "Maybe I'll fight."   "I'm at ease, all's well."

Don't Leave Pets in Parked Cars!

Many well-meaning pet owners who take their animals shopping with them are shocked to learn—too late—that animals left inside a parked car can suffer brain damage or die in a very short time. Leaving the windows open doesn't necessarily mean your pet will survive. The heat radiating from a parking lot's surface on an 85-degree day will cause the inside temperature of the car to reach 102–104 degrees in *ten minutes* even if the windows are partly rolled down for air circulation. Within fifteen to thirty minutes the temperature will reach 120 degrees. In the sun, temperatures will reach 160 degrees in a very short time.

Dogs and cats can withstand a temperature of 107–108 degrees only for an extremely short time before suffering irreparable brain damage and—very quickly—death. They do not perspire as people do. The enclosed car's overheated air prevents the animal from cooling itself as it normally does through panting.

Symptoms of heatstroke include heavy panting, vomiting, glazed eyes, reddish purple tongue color, and convulsions which lead to collapse. If your pet shows any of these signs, it is urgent that you *immediately* immerse the animal in cool water or spray it gently with a hose. Apply cold cloths or ice packs to its head and neck and under the tail until body temperature is lowered. Then take the pet to a veterinarian. Don't wait—this is an emergency! Brain damage from heatstroke is irreversible.

Make it a rule *never* to leave a pet in a car parked in the sun—even if the temperature outside is cool. And never leave a pet in a car parked in the *shade* if the temperature outside is above 70 degrees.

Dog Heroes

Animals are the best kinds of heroes. They're selfless, they act without concern for their own welfare, and they never brag. If modesty is the better part of heroism, then animals are heroes of the first magnitude. Surely they deserve more than the medals and silver bowls they receive each year via the hero award programs that recognize their acts. At the very least, they deserve our admiration and respect—and we'd be hard-pressed to deny that any one of our animal heroes deserves a pat on the head from its master and a heartfelt "well done, thou good and faithful servant."

Champ and **Buddy,** two dogs from Dickinson, North Dakota, were named national heroes in the Ken-L Ration Dog Hero of the Year contest in 1986. Champ, a seven-year-old Cairn terrier, and Buddy, a three-year-old mixed breed owned by Harvey and

Anneliese Schmidt, were honored for helping save a man pinned under a 2,680-pound scraper tire that fell on him in an isolated warehouse. The dogs, having left their house at 2 A.M. for a brief run on a 20-below-zero night, discovered Marvin Dacar trapped in an empty warehouse near their home. He had been unloading his truck alone when one of the tires rolled over on him. Returning to the house, the dogs barked continuously to attract their owners' attention and then refused to enter the house, finally leading the Schmidts through the cold to the warehouse. It took two hours to free Marvin from under the tire. When he was rushed to the hospital for surgery doctors told him he would have died from shock and blood loss if Buddy and Champ hadn't acted so persistently and quickly. The dogs have since become, in Marvin's words, "my best friends."

Woodie, a collie mix dog from Cleveland, Ohio, saved his mistress's fiancé from drowning. Rae Ann and her fiancé, Ray, were walking in a forest preserve near a river when Ray said he'd like to take a good picture of the river. He asked Rae Ann to hold Woodie while he searched out the proper vantage point, but a few minutes later Woodie began to pull away from Rae. The dog finally broke loose and ran off in the direction Ray had gone. Rae Ann ran after her. When she reached the dog on the top of a nearby cliff, she saw Ray lying at the bottom of the cliff, eighty feet below, face down in the shallow river. Woodie had just jumped off the cliff and was beside him pulling his face out of the water. By the time Rae Ann reached the river, help had arrived. Woodie had broken his hip in his leap off the cliff. Ray was also badly injured, but he was alive, thanks to Woodie's courage. He became Ken-L Ration's Dog Hero of 1980.

Lady, a Boston terrier owned by Don Bellonio of Santa Rosa, California, was bitten by a rattlesnake while she was protecting a two-year-old child from the snake. For her courage and devotion, Lady received the 1987 William O. Stillman Award. The award is made annually "in recognition of rescue of an animal at the risk of personal danger or sacrifice and also to animals that may save human life."

Zorro, a German shepherd from Orangevale, California, received both the Stillman Award and the Ken-L Ration Dog Hero Award in 1976 for his remarkable bravery in saving his master's life. Zorro went on a hiking trip in the mountains with his owner, Mark, and some friends. As they walked along the edge of a cliff, Mark lost his balance and fell some 85 feet into a rocky river. Zorro raced to the river and pulled his master out of a swift whirlpool. As Mark reached the slippery rocks on the bank of the river he lost his balance and fell back into the river. Zorro once again pulled him out of the strong current. While one of Mark's friends went for help, Zorro slept on top of his master to keep him warm. And when help finally arrived, Zorro had to stay behind because there wasn't enough room in the rescue vehicle. When a search party went back to look for Zorro, they found him still guarding Mark's backpack beside the river.

Dory, a seeing-eye German shepherd from Palm Beach, Florida, received the William O. Stillman Award after a sighted person told her master it was okay to cross a busy street. Dory valiantly attempted to hold her master back and succeeded in saving his life, but was herself killed by an oncoming car.

Leo, a standard poodle from Hunt, Texas, took six bites from a five-and-a-half-foot rattlesnake while protecting his eleven-year-old master, Sean Callahan. Leo and Sean had gone with Sean's nine-year-old sister to play near the Guadalupe River when they stumbled upon the huge snake. Without a moment's hesitation, Leo lunged between the snake and Sean. Leo's attack on the snake nearly cost him his own life. His veterinarian called Leo's recovery "remarkable" and attributes his extraordinary will to live as a major factor in the brave dog's survival. He won the Ken-L Ration Hero Dog award in 1984.

Beggar, a St. Bernard, became his three-year-old master's hero when the little boy wandered away from his home in California. When a search was mounted, Boy Scouts found the little Bobby wandering with the dog a mile away from home. Both boy and dog were dripping wet. When Bobby took off his wet clothes, the imprints of huge teeth were obvious on his body. Bobby told his rescuers that he had fallen into a nearby river. Beggar had jumped in and picked him up with her mouth, carrying him safely to shore.

Lassie, a shetland sheepdog from California, slept in her six-year-old master's bedroom. One night little Gary became gravely ill. Lassie ran into Gary's parents' bedroom and barked loudly to wake them. When the adults paid little attention, Lassie pulled off their covers and raced around the room barking in an even louder, more frantic manner. At last, they followed the dog. She led them to Gary's bedroom where they discovered their son on the floor there told his parents that Gary might have died if the dog hadn't intervened. Lassie became the 1956 Ken-L Ration Dog Hero.

And Some Human Heroes:

Duke Suedell and **Bruce Reed** of Grand Forks, North Dakota, received a Stillman Award for rescuing a partially blind poodle trapped in ice on a river near their home.

Homer Ellett of San Francisco was credited with saving the life of a dog he saw jump out of a car window into San Francisco Bay. Both Homer and the dog survived the dramatic rescue.

Mrs. Ernest LeClair of Nassau, New York, saved the life of "Andy" the dog by giving him mouth-to-mouth resuscitation after a fire.

James Welch of Louisville, Kentucky, won the Stillman Award after he lost both arms while saving his puppy, "Smoky," from an oncoming train.

The behavior of men to animals and their behavior to each other bear a constant relationship.

—Herbert Spencer

And God spake unto Noah, and to his sons with him, saying, and I, behold, I establish my covenant with you, and with your seed after you, and with every living creature that is with you, of the fowl, of the cattle, and of every beast of the earth with you; from all that go out of the ark, to every beast of the earth.

—Genesis 9:8–10

Montmorency

by Jerome K. Jerome

To look at Montmorency you would imagine that he was an angel sent upon the earth, for some reason withheld from mankind, in the shape of a small fox terrier. There is a sort of Oh-what-a-wicked-world-this-is-and-how-I-wish-I-could-do-something-to-make-it-better-and-nobler expression about Montmorency that has been known to bring tears to the eyes of pious old ladies and gentlemen.

When first he came to live at my expense, I never thought I should be able to get him to stop long. I used to sit down and look at him, as he sat on a rug and looked up at me, and think: "Oh, that dog will never live. He will be snatched up to the bright skies in a chariot, this is what will happen to him."

But when I had paid for about a dozen chickens that he had killed; and had dragged him, growling and kickin, by the scruff of his neck, out of a hundred and fourteen street fights; and had had a dead cat brought round for my inspection by an irate female, who called me a murderer; and had been summoned by the man next door for having a ferocious dog at large, that had kept him pinned up in his own toolshed, afraid to venture his nose outside the door for over two hours on a cold night; and had learned that the gardener, unknown to myself, had won thirty shillings by backing him to kill rats against time, then I began to think that maybe they'd let him remain on earth for a bit longer, after all.

The only subject on which Montmorency and I have any serious difference of opinion is cats. I like cats; Montmorency does not. When I meet a cat, I say, "Poor Pussy!" and stoop down and tickle the side of its head; and the cat sticks up its tail in a rigid, cast-iron manner, arches its back, and wipes its nose up against my trousers; and all is gentleness and peace. When Montmorency meets a cat, the whole street knows about it; and there is enough bad language wasted in ten seconds to last an ordinary respectable man all his life, with care.

I do not blame the dog (contenting myself, as a rule, with merely clouting his head or throwing stones at him), because I take it that it is his nature. Fox terriers are born with about four times more original sin in them as other dogs are, and it will take years and years of patient effort on the part of us Christians to bring about any appreciable reformation in the rowdiness of the fox-terrier nature.

I remember being in the lobby of the Haymarket Stores one day, and all round me were dogs, waiting for the return of their owners, who were shopping inside. There were a mastiff, and one or two collies, and a Saint Bernard, a few retrievers and Newfoundlands, a boar-hound, a French poodle, with plenty of hair round its head, but mangy about the middle, a bulldog, a few Lowther Arcade sort of animals, about the size of rats, and a couple of Yorkshire tykes.

There they sat, patient, good, and thoughtful. A solemn peacefulness seemed to reign in that lobby. An air of calmness and resignation—of gentle sadness pervaded the room.

Then a sweet young lady entered, leading a meek-looking little fox terrier, and left him, chained up there, between the bulldog and the poodle. He sat and looked about him for a minute. Then he cast up his eyes to the ceiling, and seemed, judging from his expression, to be thinking of his mother. Then he yawned. Then he looked around at the other dogs, all silent, grave, and dignified.

He looked at the bulldog, sleeping dreamlessly on his right. He looked at the poodle, erect and haughty, on his left. Then, without a word of warning, without the shadow of provocation, he bit that poodle's near foreleg, and a yelp of agony rang through the quiet shades of that lobby.

The result of his first experiment seemed highly satisfactory to him, and he determined to go on and make things lively all round. He sprang over the poodle and vigorously attacked a collie, and the collie woke up, and immediately commenced a fierce and noisy contest with the poodle. Then Foxey came back to his own place, and caught the bulldog by the ear, and tried to throw him away; and the bulldog, a curiously impartial animal, went for everything he could reach, including the hall-porter, which gave that dear little terrier the opportunity to enjoy an uninterrupted fight of his own with an equally willing Yorkshire tyke.

Anyone who knows canine nature need hardly be told that, by this time, all the other dogs in the place were fighting as if their hearths and homes depended on the fray. The big dogs fought each other indiscriminately; and the little dogs fought among themselves, and filled up their spare time by biting the legs of the big dogs.

The whole lobby was a perfect pandemonium, and the din was terrific. A crowd assembled outside in the Haymarket, and asked if it was a vestry meeting; or, if not, who was being murdered, and why? Men came with poles and ropes, and tried to separate the dogs, and the police were sent for.

And in the midst of the riot that sweet young lady returned, and snatched up that sweet little dog of hers (he had laid the tyke up for a month, and had on the expression, now, of a new-born lamb) into her arms, and kissed him, and asked him if he was killed, and what those great nasty brutes of dogs had been doing to him; and he was nestled up against her, and gazed up into her face with a look that seemed to say: "Oh, I'm so glad you've come to take me away from this disgraceful scene!"

She said that the people at the stores had no right to allow great savage things like those other dogs to be put with respectable people's dogs, and that she had a great mind to summon somebody.

Such is the nature of fox terriers; and, therefore, I do not blame Montmorency for his tendency to row with cats, but he wished he had not given way to it that morning.

We were, as I have said, returning from a dip, and halfway up the High Street a cat darted out from one of the houses in front of us, and began to trot across the road. Montmorency gave a cry of joy—the cry of a stern warrior who sees his enemy given over into his hands—the sort of cry Cromwell might have uttered when the Scots came down the hill—and flew after his prey.

His victim was a large black tom. I never saw a larger cat, nor a more disreputable-looking cat. It had lost half its tail, one of its ears, and a fairly appreciable proportion of its nose. It was a long, sinewy-looking animal. It had a calm, contented air about it.

Montmorency went for that poor cat at a rate of twenty miles an hour; but the cat did not hurry up—did not seem to have grasped the idea that its life was in danger. It trotted quietly on until its would-be assassin was within a yard of it, and then it turned round and sat down in the middle of the road, and looked at Montmorency with a gentle, inquiring expression, that said:

"Yes? You want me?"

Montmorency does not lack pluck; but there was something about the look of that cat that might have chilled the heart of the boldest dog. He stopped abruptly, and looked back at Tom. Neither spoke; but the conversation that one could imagine was clearly as follows:

THE CAT: "Can I do anything for you?"

MONTMORENCY: "No—no, thanks."

THE CAT: "Don't you mind speaking, if you really want anything, you know."

MONTMORENCY: (*backing down the High Street*): "Oh no—not at all—certainly—don't you trouble. I—I'm afraid I've made a mistake. I thought I knew you. Sorry I disturbed you."

THE CAT: "Not at all—quite a pleasure. Sure you don't want anything, now?"

MONTMORENCY: (*still backing*): "Not at all, thanks—not at all—very kind of you. Good morning."

THE CAT: "Good morning."

Then the cat rose, and continued his trot; and Montmorency, fitting what he calls his tail carefully into its groove, came back to us, and took up an important position in the rear.

To this day, if you say the word "Cats!" to Montmorency, he will visibly shrink and look up piteously at you, as if to say: "Please don't."

—from *Three Men in a Boat*

If you pick up a starving dog and make him prosperous, he will not bite you. That is the principal difference between a dog and a man.
          —Mark Twain, *Pudd'nhead Wilson's Calendar*

Exploring Dogs

by Valerie Porter

Igloo was no wolf-dog—he was a fox terrier who went with Admiral Byrd on his first Antarctic expedition from 1928 to 1930. He was given lined boots, a camel-hair coat covering his legs, and a wool-lined sleeping crate at the foot of Byrd's bed. He was always game for a go at the large Eskimo dogs and "no doubt he believed he was a great fighter because we saved his life so often."

Bobbie was a young female collie. Her family moved from Ohio to a new home in Oregon which the dog had never been to. She wandered off on the journey during a stop in Indiana and turned up in Oregon three months later.

Hobo was a much-traveled dog, living up to his name. He turned up in 1957 at a railroad yard in Hopewell, Virginia, and thereafter he traveled thousands of miles either in the cab or on the cat-walks. He always returned to Hopewell as his base.

Owney did even better and in the nineteenth century was claimed to be the most traveled dog in history, according to the United States Post Office. He came in out of the cold one day as a puppy and found himself in a post office in Albany, New York, in 1888. When he got bored of watching the mail sacks being loaded on to railway cars he disappeared, but he returned and was given a collar and a tag asking postal workers to stamp on it the names of

the places he reached. He was given a lifetime pass to ride on any United States mail car. He reached Alaska in 1895, went down the Pacific Coast to Tacoma and then followed the mail sack up a gangplank in the *SS Victoria*, bound for Japan, where he was presented to the Mikado, decorated and given an honorary passport. The Emperor of China honoured him in the same fashion. He went through the Suez Canal and back across the Atlantic to his home base, having accumulated two hundred medals on his travels. He later died after a dog fight; his body was sent to a taxidermist and he was put on display in the Postal Museum, Washington, D.C., along with all his medals and stamped tags.

Retirement Homes for Animals

Pets sometimes find themselves homeless after years with a loving family because the family can no longer keep the animal for reasons that are beyond the control of the family. Older pet owners can die or become too ill to care for a loved cat or dog, or must move to a nursing home where pets are not allowed. And from time to time a stray enters our lives that we can no longer keep—but we don't want to send it to the pound to be euthanized. When pets need the love and care their owners can no longer give them, there's now a humane alternative to putting the animal to sleep: a retirement home.

Several marvelous homes are available in different parts of the country. Among the best:

Animal Haven Farm, c/o Associated Humane Societies, 124 Evergreen Ave., Newark, New Jersey 07114; (201) 824-7080. Pets live in well-cared-for facilities and have room to enjoy themselves with other animals if they're able. The cost for lifetime care in this loving atmosphere is based on the age of your pet. Good homes are sought for animals (a careful screening process is used), but if an animal is unable to be placed he can live out his life in comfort at the Farm. A tag can be ordered for each of your pets which reads: "In the event of the death of my owner, please immediately call Associated Humane Societies." The telephone number is listed. A wallet card is also provided in case you become incapacitated while away from home. As soon as they receive a call, AHS arranges for your pet to be picked up and transported to Animal Haven Farm.

Peace Plantation, P.O. Box 837, Leesburg, Virginia 22075, is a facility of the National Humane Education Society. Animals get complete care and plenty of love for the rest of their natural lives. A new Plantation facility is being planned that will shelter more animals and offer services to pet owners. Send for their quarterly journal.

Kent Animal Shelter, Inc., River Road, Calverton, New York; (516) 727-5731 provides lifetime care in a ranch setting on nearly two acres along the Peconic River. Pets receive loving care in a homelike atmosphere from "foster parents" who live at the ranch. No pet is caged; all receive complete veterinary surveillance and are allowed to live out their natural lives unless there is extreme and unbearable pain. The Shelter is self-supporting and exists through the bequests of pet owners.

Check with your local humane society or S.P.C.A. for the names of other Retirement Centers in your area. New ones are springing up regularly. Carefully check out all facilities before you decide where your pet will be happiest. If you're dealing with a center in another part of the country, ask for photos and plenty of information about the organization running the facility.

Our Dog Won't Retire

by Maynard Good Stoddard

"All of the dogs who live in America have had their work taken away," a leading obedience trainer says. "They no longer herd. They don't pull sleds. They are unemployed."

That being the case, certainly a dog 10 years of age (supposedly equivalent to 70 human years) should be all the more content to hang up his collar and call it quits. Time he began bringing his so-called master his slippers instead of running off with the man's shoe and burying it under the lilac bush. Time he spent his declining years lying at his master's feet and dreaming of that flirtatious Chihuahua that lived next door to our apartment in Indianapolis. Or perhaps those exciting winter mornings when he would close the front door on old lord and master, outside in his pajamas to pick up the *Indianapolis Star*. Time, at least, he gave lord and master a few minutes to meditate on the well-formed blonde who owned the Chihuahua next door.

Giving Brutus the benefit of the doubt, we may have to take some of the blame for moving from that apartment to these 13 hilltop "achers" at Freedom, Indiana. After years of confinement, Brutus seemingly can't do enough to show his appreciation for being sprung.

Thanks to his industrious digging in the garden for moles, he has relieved me of much of the drudgery of hoeing—he digs up plants, roots and all. By electing to take his siestas in the cool of the flower beds, he has equally relieved Lois—there isn't much she can do for a flat flower. Mulching the lawn with organic matter, which includes cow skulls, chicken carcasses, and choice bits from the trash burner, is another duty Brutus has accepted without prompting. And then there's the way he protects our home from strangers by planting both feet on their shoulders and trying to slobber them to death.

Foolishly, we had thought our mornings of heaving ourselves out of the sack at 5:45 were over. Brutus, however, concerned we have forgotten to set the alarm, begins to call attention to our oversight at 5:30 sharp. A believer in the adage "If at first you don't succeed," his volume increases until, by 6:00, he's into decibels that penetrate both the bed covers and the pillow now covering the master's head. Lois, only recently afflicted with an early-morning hearing problem, doesn't miss a snore.

With visions of Brutus by now standing on crossed legs and chewing on the doorknob, I leave the snug refuge of the bed, whack my knee on the glass top of the coffee table (a tradition), perhaps step barefoot on a T-bone or a cat-food can he sneaked in the night before, and turn him loose. It is little consolation in the pale light of dawn to observe that his urgency has nothing to do with his favorite tree. Instead, it's either to chase Flaky, Lois' cat, up a clothesline post or to dash over and wake up Gail Abrell's rooster, in case it has overslept.

Having read that older people require fewer calories than the gung-ho generation, I had thought this would apply to older dogs as well. In fact, our reduced food budget called for us to eat less and for Brutus to live pretty much off the land—by bagging a moose, a deer, or the neighbors' chickens, in season—with maybe a few orts (as the crossword-puzzle people label table scraps) for dessert.

However, whether it's the early-morning rising or the extra exercise I get from replanting the garden, picking up the litter on the lawn, and dashing out to unplant Brutus' big feet from the shoulders of strangers, I am eating more than I ever did in the apartment. As for that dog, the closest he comes to living off the land is stealing eggs out of the neighbors' chicken coops. We are now buying dry dog food by the 50-pound sack and canned dog food by the case. He also makes sure that the cat's dish and her milk saucer are kept clean. We make restitution for the neighbors' eggs once a week.

Ignoring the weight—at least 40 pounds—of her female Garfield cat, Snowflake (or Flaky, as I have nicknamed the spoiled beast), Lois had the audacity to remark, "Your dog is getting fat. From now on it's dry dog food only!"

For my rebuttal, I had only to remind her of Cookie, the dog we had acquired in Florida while I was seeking my fortune as a free-lance writer. I had done so well that at one point our larder was reduced to a barrel of home-canned peaches, the last of our estate shipped down from Michigan.

"A dog that won't eat canned peaches can't be very hungry," we kept telling ourselves. But on the third day of this fare, after tying Cookie to the back bumper and walking into town, we returned to find that Cookie had somehow discovered that the trailer was made of some sort of edible composition. He had edibled a hole big enough to crawl through and was contentedly dozing on our bed.

Another thing—our meals here were to be casual, leisurely, even candlelight affairs upon occasion. But Brutus has little patience when it comes to waiting for his orts. And for all the miracles that compose the human anatomy, the digestive system refuses to function efficiently with an impatient mastiff drooling at the diner's elbow.

We tried exiling him to the outside during mealtime; he stared at us accusingly through the window. We pulled the shade; he scratched on the door. We tied him to the elm tree; he cut loose with howling that brought the neighbors. We untied him and gave him a bone; he dug out the last of my radishes and buried them again in the garden. He was back scratching on the door before I could regain my seat at the table.

Synchronizing his mealtime with ours proved equally brilliant. Somewhere in Brutus' roots there must be a tad of hamster blood that allows him to store food in a pouch: Not even a dog his size can ingest food and be back at my elbow that fast. It wouldn't make any difference if he *had* just bagged a moose; he begins the pitiful moan that can only be interpreted as "Just a crust, master—please don't let your faithful old dog starve to death in this land of plenty."

When this fails, his next intonement is even more definite: "Come on, fatso, just one little bite of that hamburger, that's all I'm asking . . . help! . . . HElp! . . . HELP!" To spare the neighbors another trip, I give him the rest of my hamburger and blow out the candles, and another quiet dinner is shot down.

Our dreams of long, leisurely evenings have fared no better. With the kids safely flown from the nest, we had thought our nights of waiting up and worrying were over. We had taken for granted that at age 70 Brutus' romantic rompings would be on the wane, if not waned altogether. Instead, he seems to be just hitting his stride.

At first, we sat up and waited and worried. Then we got smart and didn't let him out in the evening. That worked fine until we went to bed. When the wailing began carrying to the Abrells', I got out of bed and led him outside. One night I tried tying him to the clothesline; this cost us a new clothesline. Then I tied him to the clothesline post; this cost me the effort of not only resetting the clothesline post but also replacing the trash burner, which was wiped out when he shot past with the post bouncing along on the end of the rope.

I finally invested in a dog harness and anchored him to the elm tree. The tree stayed in the ground, but dog harnesses evidently aren't made the way they used to be. We expect to be on the receiving end of a paternity suit any day now.

"Maybe if you can get him tired out before bedtime," Lois suggested one night while esconced safely in bed. So Brutus and I went outside for a few games of Fetch the Ball, or, as we played it, Knock the Master Flat. An hour later, I fell asleep on the sofa while taking off my shoes. Brutus seized the opportunity to curl up on the bed next to Lois. She didn't know the difference until he began licking the cold cream off her face. I *never* do that.

"Maybe it's just a phase," was Lois' next bit of encouragement, again from the bed. "And there must be plenty of people who stay up and watch Johnny Carson who don't even have a dog."

So now I'm watching Carson nightly and hoping the "phase" will peter out before I do. If Brutus doesn't retire soon, it's back to Indianapolis for us. I was getting more sleep on the job than I'm getting now. Besides, they don't allow dogs in the company cafeteria. And who knows, once back there I may be able to lay up a few cases of dog food for a rainy day.

What Does It Cost to Own a Dog?

Estimates of the cost of feeding a small (ten-pound) dog range from $125 to $200 per year. A medium-sized, forty-pound dog will eat $375 to $475 worth of food, and an average eighty-pounder will consume from $500 to $700.

Veterinary bills in the first year of a dog's life generally run about $200. The next eight to ten years' vet bills will average less than $150 a year, barring accidents or serious illness.

Total costs to own a small dog (including food, boarding when you're on vacation, grooming, licenses, toys, and vet bills) will usually run from $3,500 to $4,000 over a ten-year life span. A large dog will cost $8,000 to $10,000. The most costly dog will give its owners love, companionship, pleasure, and comfort for about $2.80 per day, or 11 cents per hour over its lifetime.

Saintly Connections

by Valerie Porter

Saint Bernard: The Hospice du Grand Saint Bernard, one of the highest human habitations in Europe, was originally the site of a temple to Jupiter. Bernard of Menthon rebuilt it as a refuge offering hospitality to pilgrims, and it was here that the well-known breed of large mountain dogs was developed to help guide travelers on their way.

Saint Benignus and **Saint Wendelin:** In medieval art a dog represented fidelity. Each of these saints is portrayed with a dog at his feet.

Saint Dominic: A dog is often portayed carrying a lighted torch to guide Saint Dominic.

Saint Hubert: The patron saint of hunters gave his name to one of the early breeds of hound. Saint Hubert was a passionate deer hunter but he never hunted again after he beheld the apparition of a stag with the image of Christ on the cross between its antlers.

Saint Roch: Saint Roch's dog was the epitome of faithfulness. The saint was smitten with the plague while he was tending victims of that terrible disease; he took refuge in the depths of the forest, and the dog brought him his daily bread and licked his plague sores.

Wordsworth's Dog

Lie here, without a record of thy worth,
Beneath a covering of the common earth!
It is not from unwillingness to praise,
Or want of love, that here no Stone we raise;
More thou deserv'st; but *this* Man gives to Man,
Brother to brother, *this* is all we can.
Yet they to whom thy virtues made thee dear
Shall find thee through all the changes of the year:
This Oak points out thy grave; the silent tree
Will gladly stand a monument of thee.
I grieved for thee, and wished thy end were passed;
And willingly have laid thee here at last:
For thou hadst lived till everything that cheers
In thee had yielded to the weight of years;
Extreme old age had wasted thee away,
And left thee but a glimmering of the day;
Thy ears were deaf, and feeble were thy knees,—
I saw thee stagger in the summer breeze.
Too weak to stand against its sportive breath,
And ready for the gentlest stroke of death.
It came, and we were glad; yet tears were shed;
Both Man and Woman wept when Thou were dead;
Not only for a thousand thoughts, that were,
Our household thoughts, in which thou hadst thy share;
But for some precious boons vouchsafed to thee,
Found scarcely anywhere in like degree!
For love, that comes to all—the holy sense,
Best gift of God—in thee was most intense;
A chain of heart, a feeling of the mind,
A tender sympathy, which did thee bind
Not only to us Men, but to thy Kind;
Yea, for thy Fellow-brutes in thee we saw
The soul of Love. Love's intellectual law;—
Hence, if we wept, it was not done in shame;
Our tears from passion and from reason came,
And, therefore, shalt thou be an honoured name.

—William Wordsworth

Dog Gone

by George Stanley

My great-grandfather looked as if he were holding back tears as he stood in the living room and stared out the window. I had never seen him so sad. "What's wrong, Grampa?" I asked.

He looked down at me, then back out the window. "Buck is gone," he said, his voice cracking with emotion. "He's not coming back."

I was less surprised by the content of this statement than by its timing. Ol' Buck had been dead for years. It occurred to me that maybe Gramps meant to say that King, our current black Lab, wouldn't be coming home. "King has taken off before," I said. "Sometimes for a week or more."

My oldest living ancestor shook his head. "It's different this time. I just have a feeling. . . ."

It wasn't unusual for my great-grandfather to get these "feelings." One time, for instance, when King was a puppy, Gramps spoke of a "powerful feeling" he had that the dog was destined to become a field champion retriever. The mere mention of that prediction still sends Dad into seizures of laughter. Both my parents, in fact, seemed to appreciate Great-Grampa's extrasensory perceptions for their entertainment value. I took his feelings much more seriously, however, because I'd seen some of them come true.

There was the time, for example, when Gramps and I were walking in the woods, and he stopped suddenly and sniffed the air. "I have a feeling a wee leprechaun has made his home in these woods," he said. "Let's see if we can find his pot o' gold!" We searched behind bushes and beneath boulders for 15 minutes. Then Grampa reached deep into a hollow tree. "I think I've found it!" he said.

"We found a pot o' gold! We found a pot o' gold!" I shouted with glee. My dance ended abruptly when Grampa's hand emerged from the hole clutching nothing more than a half-emptied bottle.

"*Ahh,*" Gramps said grinning, as he unscrewed the cap. "This is truly a magical treasure." He sat down, took a long pull and wiped his mouth with his sleeve. "A leprechaun left this here, I'm sure of it," he said. "Must be from his private stock." He took another hefty swig and then looked at me sternly. "Don't breathe a word of this to anyone," he whispered. "That leprechaun will be back, and we don't want someone else to get his gold, do we?"

I had searched the clearing on many occasions since—some times with Great-Grampa, sometimes with King, sometimes by myself. Though I never found the wee leprechaun's pot o' gold, I did unearth at least half a dozen bottles from his private stock, so I knew he was there. And I was one of just two people aware of his presence, thanks to that strange feeling Great-Grampa had during our walk.

Now Grampa's sixth sense was telling him that dear King was gone for good. As the sorrow of that inevitably struck, I tilted back my head to keep the tears from spilling out. Grampa dabbed at his eyes and looked down at the floor. "This was Buck's favorite spot," he sniffed. "The old boy used to lie here in the sun and rest up for our long days afield."

I nodded the affirmative, for King had indeed spent the vast bulk of each day lying log-stiff on the very spot where we were standing. One time, in fact, he had lain here for two days without twitching a muscle. We thought he'd died, until Great-Grampa grabbed the carcass by the tail to drag it outside. But then! Well, a comparison to Dr. Jekyll and Mr. Hyde wouldn't do justice to the change that occurred in King. You should've seen poor Grampa's arm! That was the day King earned his nickname, Chainsaw. As Dad was fond of pointing out, that nickname also applied to the way King handled birds in the field.

As memories of the big Lab overwhelmed me, I bent my head in sorrow only to see the dusty image of King that had been permanently etched onto the carpet. Ever since the chainsaw massacre, Mom had been careful to vacuum around our loving pet. "Better to let sleeping dogs lie," she said.

The doorbell bing-bonged Grampa and me away from our melancholy reverie. Gramps strode over to the front door and opened it. There was no one there. He stepped outside and looked around. "Hallo!" he hollered, "Hallo!" He came back in and slammed the door. "Must've been a wrong number," he grumbled.

"Think someone might be at the back door?" I asked. Grampa tousled my hair and smiled. "You're not nearly as stupid as that teacher's been telling your mom," he said with pride.

In the back hallway we found Mom talking to one of the neighbors. She turned to us with worried eyes. "Mrs. Miller says there's an awful stench coming from the bushes out back."

Mrs. Miller nodded. "Smells like something died down there," she said.

Great-Grampa's eyes widened. "Buck!" he cried, then dashed past Mrs. Miller and out the door. I tore after him. We were both stopped short by the reeking black mass of unidentifiable scum that lay in a hollow among the tall lilac shrubs.

I suddenly remembered that this was the place where Hog Hansen and I had torched a 10-pound bag of potatoes only a week earlier. Hog had been hungry and had pilfered the potatoes from the Millers' garage. He figured that instead of peeling and slicing the potatoes individually, we could simply pour gas on the whole batch and cook them all at once. Unfortunately, Hog's potato flambé, once we got it extinguished, looked nowhere near edible.

King, however, might have seen things differently, I thought to myself. The worse something smelled, the better he seemed to like it. Could King have come across the rotten potatoes, eaten one and died on the spot? If so, it would mean that I had unwittingly helped poison our prize Lab!

I heard Gramps mumbling something about a decent burial. He looked at me and said, "Run and fetch a garbage bag, and scoop Buck inside it. I'll get his personal belongings. We'll meet in the field over yonder. There's pheasant in that field; Buck should like it there."

An indifferent person might have fainted at the thought of scraping up those rancid remains. But King had been a friend of mine, so I tackled the job bravely. Still, the tears were flowing freely as I carried the body bag through the Millers' yard to the field beyond.

There I found Grampa holding a spade in one hand and a Bible in the other. He was trying simultaneously to dig a hole and read from the book of Psalms, but was having little success at either. So he handed me the shovel and instructed me on just how wide, long and deep to dig the hole.

As I started to dig, Great-Grampa sat on the grass and closed his Bible. A sad smile formed on his ancient visage. "Remember the long hours we spent in this field training Buck?" he said. "It sure paid off though, didn't it?"

I nodded. King had been a fantastic hunting dog. He always stood up and barked to warn us when birds were coming in. He even retrieved a number of the ducks we shot (though not an especially large number), despite my great-grandfather's unorthodox training techniques.

An ardent believer in hard-nosed discipline, Great-Grampa

beamed in a peculiar way whenever he got the chance to administer some. I thought back to that day when we taught King how to jump a fence. The low garden fence in the Millers' backyard didn't suit Grampa; he searched until he found an electrified fence—the kind that coldcocked cattle. Big King looked a little nervous on his approach, but he gave it his best shot, and his forelegs cleared the height with room to spare. But then his undersides brushed that wire ever so slightly, and he howled like a wolf at the moon. Nearly flew to the moon, too, before landing at a full gallop.

King wouldn't jump any more fences on that day, of course. If he was within earshot, he wasn't heeding our calls. Great-Grampa took off his jacket and spread it on the ground. "An old trainer's trick," he said with a wink, "the dog will be lying here tomorrow."

King wasn't lying on Grampa's coat the next day. But he had left a rather poignant sign that he'd stopped by. When he finally wandered home a few days later, Grampa rubbed the dog's muzzle in the jacket. King probably didn't learn much from the incident, especially since Gramp's coat had already been dry-cleaned. But Grampa was right about one thing: We never had to worry about King clearing fences in the field—he didn't come within 100 yards of one again.

As King's grave grew deeper, I began to fling the diggings over my shoulder. "You dimwitted ying-yang!" Great-Grampa shouted. "Don't toss the dirt! What do you think we're going to cover him up with?"

Moments later, my great-grandfather's eyes moistened once again. He coughed a soft little chuckle. "Remember the time Buck crashed through the ice on Victoria Bay to fetch that big canvasback I crumpled?" he said, shaking his head. "The big fella must have retrieved 30 ducks that day!"

Now I had my doubts that Buck had ever performed such a feat, and I knew for a fact that King hadn't. Actually, I couldn't remember a time when King willingly entered the water after Labor Day. I did recall one late November hunt, however, when Gramps knocked down a merganser and commanded King to fetch. Instead, the Lab lay down in the blind and licked his paws. As King's feet got cleaner, Grampa's face grew redder and his voice got louder. Finally, Gramps flung down his gun, grabbed the dog by the neck and hurled him over the blind, screaming, "FETCH, you lily-livered fu-fu!"

Always one to hold a grudge, King swam skillfully through our decoy spread, dragging three long blocks back to the blind. If you count the wooden birds, I guess you *could* say King hauled in 30 ducks that day.

I paused, leaned against the shovel and wiped the sweat from my brow. It wasn't long before I noticed Great-Grampa glaring at me. "That ain't deep enough!" he snapped. "We don't want people trippin' over him, do we? Now get the lead out!"

I went back to work, shoveling more furiously than ever. At last, after what seemed like days of digging, I finished the ditch to Great-Grampa's satisfaction. Exhausted, I picked up the garbage bag and dropped it into the abyss. Grampa looked at me with disgust. "That's a Labrador retriever, not a sack of potatoes," he scolded. "The least you could do is show him some respect!"

Grampa threw in some of King's personal effects—his food dish, retrieving dummy and heartworm pills. Then, as I filled in the hole as best I could, Grampa recited a poem he had composed, titled "Ode to Winchester Buckingham Rex."

> *Winchester Buckingham Rex was the name*
> *But good friends called you Buck.*
> *A master retriever of all types of game:*
> *Grouse, goose, dove, turkey, duck.*
>
> *We traveled many a dirt road together,*
> *From sunrise to sunset,*
> *Flushed all types of feather in all kinds of weather;*
> *It's autumn in heaven, I bet!*
>
> *You never won a field trial*
> *But to us you were The Champ,*
> *Who lived his life in great style*
> *Right till God snuffed out the lamp.*

A bitter wind blew in from the northwest and surrounded my body like an invisible glacier. It began to rain. Great-Grampa closed his eyes and asked for silence. I shut my eyes, too, but couldn't keep my teeth from chattering.

At first I thought the scratching noises at my feet were caused by the rain against the earth. But rain had never kicked up dirt on my pant legs before. I cracked open an eye and what did I behold but Big King, in the flesh, digging up his own grave!

"Grampa," I shouted, "Look!"

My great-grandfather opened his eyes. His wrinkled face filled up with childlike wonder. "If that don't beat all," he said. "The rascal has arisen from the dead!"

Our tail-wagging ghoul reached into the buried treasure and sank his teeth into the putrid black rot we had just eulogized. Great-Grampa grabbed King by the collar and dragged him toward the house. "Pick up Buck's things out of that crud," he shouted over his shoulder. "And hurry home—it's raining out."

As the two of them ambled away, I heard Great-Grampa say, "I knew you'd come back to us, boy. I just had the feeling."

There's a word or two to be said about my great-grandfather's feelings. I just have to be careful never to say those words in front of Mom.

The Psychologist Had Dog Breath

An increasing number of psychologists and family counselors are using pets in therapy sessions with children and teenagers. It's been shown that troubled kids will open up when an animal is present; sometimes they'll talk with the pet when they refuse to talk with the counselor or with parents. One psychologist begins treatment of all her teenage patients by introducing them to her dog. Teenagers particularly seem to trust her more once they've met the dog, she says. And they're often able to express feelings indirectly through the dog that otherwise would be too painful to discuss. For example, a boy might say, "Your dog looks lonely," but what he's really saying is, "I'm lonely." Pets also seem to have an uncanny ability to make even the saddest child smile.

Elegy on the Death of a Mad Dog

Good people all, of every sort,
  Give ear unto my song;
And if you find it wondrous short,
  It cannot hold you long.

In Islington there was a man
  Of whom the world might say,
That still a godly race he ran—
  Whene'er he went to pray.

A kind and gentle heart he had,
  To comfort friends and foes;
The naked every day he clad—
  When he put on his clothes.

And in that town a dog was found,
  As many dogs there be,
Both mongrel, puppy, whelp, and hound,
  And curs of low degree.

This dog and man at first were friends;
  But when a pique began,
The dog, to gain his private ends,
  Went mad, and bit the man.

Around from all the neighboring streets
  The wondering neighbors ran,
And swore the dog had lost his wits,
  To bite so good a man!

The wound it seemed both sore and sad
  To every Christian eye:
And while they swore the dog was mad,
  They swore the man would die.

But soon a wonder came to light,
  That showed the rogues they lied:—
The man recovered of the bite,
  The dog it was that died!
                   —Oliver Goldsmith

These Days Animals Are Talking Like E. F. Hutton

by Richard Wolkomir

Vice President George Bush's cocker spaniel, C. Fred Bush, has published his first book, *C. Fred's Story*, and it's a shot in the arm for all of us who rap with our pets. Like most celebrity autobiographies, it's an as-told-to, dictated to the Vice President's wife, Barbara. And it has all enthusiasts of animal-human dialogue applauding or, depending on species, wagging their tails and barking.

It seems that whenever C. Fred's picture appeared in the papers, people wrote to him. Mrs. Bush would type up his replies and mail them off, with a book the natural next step.

C. Fred's communicativeness may seem mystifying. But pet owners know animals have an eloquent vocabulary of yawns, yips, wags, whines, scratches, back rolls and withering glares when dinner is late. Interpreting these signals, owners can speak for their pets.

We had a typical exchange last evening with our own black mongrel, Sam, when he arrived in the kitchen after a long snooze in the sun room. It went like this—

Husband: Sam wants you to feed him.

Wife: Not at all. He's looking at you and wagging his tail. He says he wants *you* to feed him.

Husband: Sam says it's my turn to cook dinner, so it's only fair you open his can.

Wife: Sam says I fed him yesterday.

Husband: Sam says you can always tell your real friends.

Sam: Woof!

Sam, incidentally, addresses all adult humans as "Mr." or "Mrs." as in "Sam says 'Hello, Mr. Porter—is that Spot I smell on your knee?' " But a large malamute of my acquaintance, Tonto, who shares digs with a young attorney named Andy, is on a first-name basis with everyone. The other day his owner and I walked into the house and Tonto woofed, which I was told meant: "Hi, Andy—want to see me do my tricks?"

All this, to skeptics, is just so much back-fence yowling. As Bertrand Russell once sniffed: "No matter how eloquently a dog may bark, he cannot tell you that his parents were poor but honest." True. Gazing deeply into the brown eyes of your English setter, you can only guess what is going on in there. It might be a canine version of "How do I love thee? Let me count the ways." But then it might be merely some dim, inchoate yearning for Ken-L Ration.

Yet, people who palaver with their pets are not dotty exceptions. A Utah State University study reveals that 90 percent of all pet owners regularly chat with their dogs, cats and birds. And 73 percent are convinced their pets talk back. Nor is the notion of such a dialogue devoid of scientific backing. Biologists at Dartmouth College and the University of Washington have discovered that even willows and maples send warning signals to grovemates with airborne chemicals when they are under caterpillar attack. If mere plants communicate, can animals be mute? In fact, a number of biologists believe that the lower orders may be almost as gabby as we are.

Ants, for instance, gesture to assign hill-keeping chores. Honeybees direct hivemates to nectar-rich flowers by performing a hexapodal tap dance. And University of California ethologists say African vervet monkeys have wordlike warning cries—one scream means "snake," another "eagle."

At Purdue University, biologist Irene Pepperberg is studying a gray parrot that can count and identify colors. In his book *Non-Human Thought*, Jacques Graven tells of another gray parrot, Jaco, who lived in Salzburg from 1827 to 1854. He greeted visitors in the morning with "Good day," and in the afternoon with "Good afternoon." When his master went out, Jaco would say, "God be with you." When Jaco's owner brought home a bird and it sang for the first time, Jaco turned to it and said kindly, "Bravo, little one, bravo."

Another famous parrot, Coco, would declare: "Coco wants to and must eat now!" Once an old major tried to teach Coco tricks, saying, "Get up on the perch, Coco." After a disgusted silence, Coco guffawed and said: "Major, up on the perch, Major!"

Scientists have spent whole careers trying to talk to dolphins, patiently teaching sign language to apes. Perhaps impelled by the loneliness of man's long evolutionary voyage, they seek an encouraging word from the kin we left behind, confabulating with the likes of "Nim Chimpsky," an educated chimpanzee, researchers optimistically named after Harvard's leading linguistics expert. Trained simians, though in some ways the most gifted, do not always have smooth conversational sailing, however. An Atlanta chimp, Lana, confronted with her first cucumber, signaled: "Banana which is green." But psychologist Francine Patterson encouragingly reports that *her* pupil, Koko, a gorilla, can be disconcertingly human: "She loves an argument, and . . . will lie her way out of a jam."

Now I wish Dr. Patterson would talk to my dog, Sam. Every night he barks for 11 minutes at the potted cactus in the dining room, and I'd darned well like to know what he's saying.

The great pleasure of a dog is that you may make a fool of yourself with him and not only will he not scold you, but he will make a fool of himself too.
                                                        —*Samuel Butler*

A Wary Pet Owner's Guide to Everything From Gerbils to Restaurant Lobsters

by Dave Barry

The first pet I ever had was an ant colony my mother gave me for Christmas when I was ten. This just goes to show the kind of deranged gifts people buy under threat of Christmas. Our house was already overrun with ants, and my mother hated them. She'd spend hours in the kitchen, whapping at them with a broom.

But those were ordinary house ants; the ones she bought me were professional, educated ants. The idea was that I would feed them sugar water, and they would teach me the wonders of nature by doing whatever ants do when they're in the privacy of their homes, as opposed to when they're carrying off disgusting little pieces of old hamburger. So I gave them names, fed them sugar water, and after about two days they all died—probably from tooth decay. I recall being upset at the time, which is pretty ironic because I thought nothing of mashing the house ants with hard-cover books.

That's the whole thing about a pet: The instant you give an animal a name, it ceases to be a random part of nature, and you no longer feel comfortable mashing or eating it. Take cows. We think nothing of eating them when they're in the form of roast beef, but if you ever spend a few minutes alone with an actual

in-person cow, you find yourself petting it and even trying to hold a conversation with it.

My sister Kate used to form this kind of attachment to animals very rapidly. Our family would go to a seafood restaurant with one of those tanks containing a bunch of lobsters staring at you and wearing handcuffs, and before long Kate would have given them names. She'd lean over the tank, chatting with them, and pretty soon the other diners would stop eating. They'd be staring at their plates, wondering what name Kate would have given *their* lobsters. Kate's a vegetarian now.

Thanks to my sister, we had a large assortment of pets when we were kids. We had several of those fluffy, silly little animals such as hamsters, gerbils and rabbits that do nothing but sit around looking terrified and pooping. We never kept them very long. Kate would start to feel sorry for them being stuck in the cage all the time, so eventually she'd let them out, and they'd scuttle across the lawn and into the woods. She thought she was doing them a great favor, but they probably didn't last long out there, nosing around in the forest floor in their wimpy little way, looking for food pellets like the ones they always got back home.

Our other major childhood pets were of the reptile variety, such as snakes, toads and salamanders. But even Kate never formed any meaningful relationships with them. Reptiles are what scientists call "cold-blooded" animals, which means that all they ever think about is murder. You know those Japanese horror films produced in the 1950's, the ones in which there is some kind of terrible atomic accident and the radiation makes reptiles grow to the size of the U.S. Treasury Building? Did you ever notice that the first thing these reptiles always do is go to the nearest city and start knocking over subway trains and eating people? Well, that's the dream of all reptiles. If you keep a pet lizard, it will just sit there in the cage, staring at you all day in a cold-blooded manner with those beady little eyes. Its single thought is: "I hope today's the day. I hope there's an atomic accident and I get bathed in radiation; then I'm gonna eat you. Hahahahahahaha!" It's a chilling thing to watch, believe me.

Turtles are the only exception to my Reptile Rule. They make loyal, warm and loving pets. I know this because two years ago I ran over a turtle named Bob with my lawnmower. (My son, who was then two and could receive signals from outer space, informed me with great confidence that the turtle's name was Bob.) Now, I didn't run over him on purpose, you understand;

I have enough trouble keeping my lawnmower going without clogging it up with turtles. Bob was unhurt, though, because Mother Nature has equipped turtles with hard shells to protect them from lawnmowers. In fact, Bob seemed to take a real shine to us after that incident, and he hung around our lawn for an entire summer, which I think was warm and loving behavior for a turtle. (Or maybe the blades had taken his legs off. It was hard to tell; I was afraid to mow the lawn after that so the grass got pretty high.)

Based on my credentials as the owner of a great many animals, I'd have to say that the very best kind of pet is a dog. When I say ''dog,'' I mean a DOG, which is a large, bounding type of salivating animal with bad breath, *not* those squeaky little things that sit on people's laps and wear sweaters and go into frenzies of excitement at the sound of their own parasites. Zoologists tell us that these are not really dogs at all. They are members of the pillow family.

The thing I like about most dogs is that they listen to you. I can spend hours talking to my German shepherd, Shawna, explaining my views on world affairs. She drinks in every word. I only wish I could hear what she's thinking:

ME: You know, Shawna, our involvement in Central America has me very concerned.

MY DOG: I wonder if he's going to give me some food.

ME: I mean, the parallels with Vietnam are positively eerie.

MY DOG: Maybe he'll give me some food now.

ME: Of course, there's no denying that the Cubans are actively involved.

MY DOG: Any minute now he's going to go in the kitchen and get me some food.

In my experience, cats rarely show this kind of interest in world affairs. And if a cat likes you, it shows its affection by sinking its claws deep into your flesh and trying to climb up your leg so it can do God-knows-what to your face. So I never had a really positive relationship with a cat.

I also have trouble with the idea of having a horse as a pet. Horses have enormous bodies with hard feet that could easily stomp a person into the consistency of grits. And you can never trust a horse because you can't look it right in the eyes. A horse has eyes about the size of cue balls, and they're located on opposite sides of its head, sometimes as much as several feet apart. So while one eye is gazing at you in a friendly and Trigger-like way, the other eye, over where you can't see it, could have a shrewd and calculating look, the look of an animal that's thinking. "What would happen to me if I stomped him to death?"

I've also learned to rule out fish as pets because every time I've ever had them the same thing always happens. I put them in the water, and they start doing what fish always do: look for a way out of the tank. They swim to one end and say to themselves: "Nope! Not here!" Then they swim to the other end and say, "Nope! Guess I'll try the other end!" And so on, hundreds of thousands of times a day, day in and day out, until they get deadly fish rot and die.

Every five years or so, my wife and I have a seizure of optimism and decide to try tropical fish again. We spend $50 on fish, fish food, medicine, filters, and special fish gravel. Then we put the water in the tank and adjust the temperature and the pH (whatever that is) because it has to be just so, or your fish will die (or so they tell you at the fish store). You wonder how these fish survive in their natural tropical environment, with plain old natural gravel and nobody to adjust the water temperature and pH for them.

Then we put in the fish, give them names, and soon come to love them as members of the family. One day we notice that Big-Tail Bob's fins are starting to rot away. So we put in some medicine, but before long, the rot has attacked them all, and some of them are swimming upside down.

Finally, the fish have no fins at all, just their little central bodies, and we just can't stand it anymore, watching them flop around bereft of dignity. So with heavy hearts we put them down the garbage disposal and put the tank back in the basement and swear we will never, ever, try to have fish again. And we don't— until the next seizure of optimism strikes us.

So, all things considered, I would say that my only really successful attempt at pet-owning has been my dog. Sure, she'll never be a great conversationalist, but she's my most faithful companion. When I'm feeling depressed, when the so-called "intelligent" human beings in my life have let me down, when it seems as though I have no friends, I can always count on Shawna to somehow sense that I need comforting. She'll nose the door open, pad into the room, lie down next to me, and start heaving on the carpet.

Earl Holliman, President, Actors and Others for Animals

Earl Holliman and his friend Katie of the "Actors and Others for Animals" organization. The group is very active in medical aid to sick and injured animals, spaying and neutering programs, and other issues related to animal welfare. Information about membership is available from A.O.A., 5510 Cahuenga Blvd., No. Hollywood, California 91601.

Miracle Man

by Deb Lawrence

"He's just a dog. Forget him and buy another one." That's what people said when Vene, our Miniature Schnauzer, was stolen from our yard. The stinging in my eyes and the tight feeling in my throat wouldn't let me answer as I thought about this beloved member of our family who had been our constant companion. My mind filled with painful memories.

I had bought Vene after a car accident killed my husband and left Rhonda, my 10-year-old daughter, in a coma for almost a year. Doctors predicted she would never regain consciousness, never talk or walk again. Thankfully, doctors are not always right. Rhonda regained consciousness and learned to walk with the aid of a walker, but she couldn't speak. She learned sign language so we could communicate.

Because Rhonda wasn't able to attend school, we took a few months to tour the country in our motor home. One day, when we stopped at a shopping mall in Colorado, Rhonda spotted a pet store. "Please," she signed, "let's go in." Reluctantly, I said we could go in for a few minutes as long as she realized we couldn't buy anything.

All the animals were adorable, but the Miniature Schnauzer had eyes that pleaded with us to take him. His busy little paws scratched rapidly at the wire cage. I walked away, but Rhonda didn't follow. When I glanced back and saw her hands trembling on her walker, I began to worry. "Come on, Rhonda," I urged. She didn't move, but her lips were now trembling as much as her hands. "Rhonda," I said with concern, "did you hear me?"

"I," she drawled, "wan' ah gog."

"You talked!" I said, tears starting in my eyes. "Tell me again, what did you say?"

"I," she said slowly but clearer, "want . . . that . . . dog."

I looked at the Miniature Schnauzer whose beady little eyes seemed to say, "See what I did. I could help her if you would give me a chance." I put my finger through the cage and gave him the best pat of gratitude the wire between us would allow. My hands were shaking, but the puppy seemed to understand.

The salesclerk was looking at us as if we had escaped from an institution. When I said, "We'd like to buy that Miniature Schnauzer," it seemed to confirm her suspicions.

"Wouldn't you like to hold him first?" she asked in the tone one uses when forced to deal with small children or imbeciles.

"No, that won't be necessary," I said. Feeling I owed her an explanation for our behavior, I told her the whole story, including the fact that Rhonda had just spoken her first words in 14 months. The clerk cried with us as we purchased the puppy.

Best of Friends

As I tenderly carried the precious cargo I had already nicknamed "my little miracle man," I thought Rhonda would throw her walker aside in her eagerness to hold him. The sparkle that had been gone so long now shone brightly in her eyes. The puppy's eyes sparkled in return. They belonged together.

The puppy never showed any of the insecurity common in most puppies. When Rhonda was seated on the sofa of the motor home, I put him down. "Call him," I urged. "Heeere . . ." was as far as she got. He ran to her and tried to jump in her lap. He seemed to know he had a mission in life and he was determined to fulfill it.

Rhonda's speech was slow and she had problems pronouncing many letters. She named the puppy Vene because it was the easiest thing for her to say. The two of them sat in the passenger seat as my copilots and rest area hawks. When she spotted the rest area signs, Rhonda's little fingers moved rapidly, informing me of the fact.

"I can't watch sign language and drive so you'll have to talk," I told her. With Vene wiggling encouragement, she gave it a determined try.

"Now!" she would exclaim as we neared the exit for the rest area.

Not once did Vene have an accident in the motor home. He seemed to understand what was expected of him before he was shown. When I was walking him, Vene maintained a perfect heel position. When Rhonda held the leash, he pulled ahead faster than she was able to move. He glanced back in encouragement as she struggled to keep up with him. Her speech was becoming more understandable and her walking more steady. In less than a week she asked me to put the walker in the back closet.

"Can't . . . keep . . . up," she said slowly.

Worried about a fall, I hesitated. I looked into Vene's eyes. He was just a puppy but he was so knowing, so mature. I put the walker away and Rhonda never used it again. She had a few falls, but always came up laughing with Vene licking her face.

As we neared home, I explained to Rhonda that Vene would be shy and afraid because he wasn't familiar with our house, and he would need reassurance. I asked her to remember his toys and bed so he would have something familiar in his new home. It was unnecessary.

As I backed into our driveway, Vene sat perched in Rhonda's lap looking out the window with his wise, knowing expression. He seemed to be thinking, "Finally, we're home."

I unlocked the door to the house and he bounded in, full of puppy curiosity. After circling the living room, he bolted for the stairs. "Poor thing," I said to Rhonda, "he's probably terrified. Did you see him run up those stairs? I'll go get him."

When I reached the landing, I saw Vene sitting inside Rhonda's room—a room that hadn't been used for nearly a year and a half. Since the accident, she had been sleeping in a hospital bed down-stairs. Of all the rooms to choose from, that puppy had gone directly to Rhonda's. I was pondering the amazing coincidence when I heard the thump . . . thump. . . . It was Rhonda coming upstairs. I wanted to shout, "No! you'll fall," but I knew it would startle her and she'd lose her balance.

Vene waited inside the door bowing repeatedly with his head on his paws and his stubby tail wagging encouragement. The instant she reached the landing, he disappeared inside her room. When Rhonda followed him, Vene barked and ran in joyous circles before he started pawing at her for attention. No one will ever convince me that puppy didn't purposefully lure her up those stairs.

Rhonda showed Vene all her little-girl treasures, and in her faltering speech she told him about the awards posted on her walls. I put Vene's bed on the floor by Rhonda's. Her final move before falling asleep was to reach up to a shelf and take down one of her stuffed animals. She carefully placed it in Vene's bed and patted him goodnight. Any other puppy would have chewed the stuffing out of that animal, but somehow I knew this one wouldn't. Not that night or any other night through the years that he slept with the stuffed puppy.

Tears of happiness slid down my cheek as I tiptoed in to kiss Rhonda goodnight. She lay peacefully asleep with the hint of a smile at the corner of her mouth. Her arm dangled over the side of the bed and rested on Vene's back. As I looked at Rhonda in the bed that had been vacant so long, Vene glanced up as if to say, "See, everything will be all right. I'm here now." Though I couldn't express the gratitude I felt for that little puppy, I knew he understood as I knelt down and scratched his chin. "Good night, my little miracle man," I whispered as I said a silent prayer for my only child and this very special puppy.

With Vene at her side, Rhonda improved so rapidly and dramatically that the school authorities suggested she return to class. Vene didn't take kindly to the yellow object that took his mistress each day, but he adjusted and learned when she would be home. Five minutes before she was due, he posted himself at the front door and waited. "Vene!" Rhonda would squeal joyfully each day when she walked in. Vene would jump and squirm in his puppy way, then drop a squeaky toy at Rhonda's feet in an invitation to play.

Three years passed and Rhonda returned to near normal. Everywhere we went, Vene went. When he heard a motor, he was ready to go. We taught him the property boundaries, which he never crossed, but we watched him closely.

On the day he was stolen, Rhonda opened the backdoor and screamed, "No, he's mine, stop!" The car was out of sight before I understood what had happened. Rhonda had a description of it so we called the sheriff. It took 30 seconds to learn they weren't interested in chasing dognappers. The date was April 16.

Hopeful Search

We offered a reward in every newspaper within 50 miles. Each day I drove the county roads hoping to catch a glimpse of either the car or Vene. At night I cried. I felt guilty for leaving him outside, guilty for teaching him to ride and, for the first time, I felt guilty for buying him. I didn't buy him for what I could do for him, but for what he could do for me . . . and Rhonda. He had accomplished a mission in life that most humans would never attain, and now he was gone.

I wondered if the people who stole him treated him well. I wondered if they loved him. I wondered if he missed us. The thought that they could have dropped him off on some lonely country road drove me to continually search for him.

Rhonda became apathetic. Her speech slowed and she lost interest in school activities. She chose to spend time alone rather than with friends. The most enthusiasm she had shown in four months was in August when the wind carried the distant sound of a dog barking. With the faith of a small child who still believes in fairies, she said, "Mom, did you hear that?" Then with a downcast look she said, "I was just hoping, that's all."

With my back turned to hide my tears, I said, "Keep hoping, Angel. He'll come back." My sole hope was that the people who stole him loved him as much as we did, or that they'd bring him back. "Anyway," I added to be convincing, "he'll run away the first chance he gets and come home." I wanted so much to believe it.

As fall approached, my hopes dimmed. What if he did try to make it home? He didn't know how to hunt for food, defend himself or keep warm in subzero temperatures. Nights were long and lonely. Lying awake, I heard sobs coming from Rhonda's room. When I walked in, her hand was resting in Vene's empty bed. "I understand, honey, I understand," was the only comfort I could offer.

Thanksgiving approached as I continued to drive the country roads. Flakes of snow began to fall and I pulled off the road and cried. "I'm losing my mind," I said to no one. "Normal people don't act this way." If anyone had overheard my one-sided conversation, I probably would not have been allowed to remain in society with normal people. Willing him to hear me, I said, "I always called you my little miracle man, Vene. You worked miracles before; you can do it again. Please, oh please, come home."

Christmas neared and Rhonda suggested we not celebrate it this year. Freezing weather came with sleet and snow. I thought of Vene's little coats and hoped he was warm. Trying to create some Christmas spirit, I asked Rhonda to help me decorate the house. As we took the decorations from the closet, the stockings fell to the floor.

"Hey, Mom," Rhonda laughed, "remember last year?" Tom, our horse, had bitten the bottom from his stocking in his eagerness to get his apples and carrots. It was so good to hear Rhonda laugh. She picked up the torn stocking. Beneath it lay the cheerful red one with "Vene" imprinted across the top. Our eyes met and we held each other while we cried.

"What will we do with it?" Rhonda sobbed. As I wiped away tears, Rhonda seemed to realize that I felt the loss as much as she did. "I know," she said, "we'll hang it. We'll hang it and he'll be home for Christmas." In a lower voice she added, "And if he's not, we'll save it until he comes home."

How long can we keep fooling ourselves, I wondered, as we hung the stockings. Rhonda looked at Vene's stocking more than I thought normal, but she tried to be cheerful. She bought him a new squeaky toy and some rawhide chewies. Still thinking about the bitter cold, I bought him a new jacket.

Christmas Present

On Christmas Eve day, Rhonda was doing some last minute shopping. I sat watching the lights blink off and on as the angel smiled down from her perch atop the tree. I thought of Christmases past and the hot dogs we wrapped and put under the tree for Vene. I was visualizing his eager eyes and stubby tail when our police scanner blared, "Has anyone reported a missing Schnauzer?" The dispatcher answered, "That's a negative."

"Well," the officer replied, "I've got one out here caught in a trap. See if you can get someone from the shelter."

With trembling hands, I dialed the Sheriff department. "That Schnauzer you were talking about, is it a male or a female?" I asked. "I have no idea," the dispatcher answered. "Would you like to hold on while I check?"

I heard her ask the officer. Hope returned as I heard him reply, "It's a male."

"Where is he?" I asked the dispatcher. "He could be mine."

She gave me the address of the officer. I drove as fast as I was safely able. The car scanner blared, "I don't know what to do with this dog, but he's going to bleed to death. Three of his toes were cut off."

A different dispatcher answered, "I just came on duty, but I know the shelter won't take him because there's no one to take care of him. Use your own judgment." Fear filled my heart as I prayed it wasn't his judgment to destroy the dog.

Officer Drake met me at the door. When I explained why I was there, he grinned. "This has got to be your dog. When he heard your car he perked right up, started whining and tried to crawl to the door."

I heard the whine and saw the blood-soaked towels. Vene was in the center wagging his stubby tail and trying to get up. After a joyful reunion, I called the vet who said the only thing I could do was elevate the leg and apply pressure. For two hours I held Vene's paw up with a cold, wet compress against his toes. Other than being weak from loss of blood, he was fine.

The bleeding had stopped and his paw had been bandaged by

the time Rhonda got home. She looked sad when she walked in. Her eyes widened and tears slid down her cheeks when she saw Vene in his bed under the Christmas tree. "Vene!" she squealed as they ran to each other. "You're back! Oh, I just knew you would be." It was the happiest Christmas of our lives.

"It's true, Mom, miracles really do happen on Christmas Eve," Rhonda said. Through tears of joy, I looked at my daughter who had been comatose for such a long time. I treasured the sound of her voice; the warmth of her gentle touch. I saw my reflection in her sparkling eyes as I said, "Miracles happen every day, Angel, you just have to believe."

Though we installed a fence for Vene around his property, he sleeps indoors. He is lying at my feet as I write. I feel his contented breathing and I think about miracles. The miracle of faith, the miracle of sight, the miracle of speech and the miracle of a man kind enough to take a bloody dog into his home on Christmas Eve. The miracle of wonder and belief in our fellow man, and the miracle of love. Yes, Rhonda, miracles do happen.

With deepest gratitute to Mr. Drake who made this happy ending possible.

Pick a Dog by Computer

Need help deciding which dog's for you? Pet food manufacturer Kal Kan Foods, Inc., has developed a computerized matching program for prospective dog owners. The free Pedigree Selectadog program asks seventeen questions about your life-style and needs, and then tells you which breeds of dog are best for your situation. Questions seek information about your age, level of activity, type of residence and yard size, time available for the pet, how much money you'll be able to spend to buy and maintain your dog adequately, and other important factors in making a wise choice. Once you've filled out the questionnaire, Kal Kan sends you a description of the dogs that will meet your needs along with information cards and a flyer with pictures of the dogs, their history, and temperaments. Send for the questionnaire from Kal Kan Foods, Inc., 3250 E. 44th Street, Vernon, California 90058. Or call toll-free: 800-Kal-Kare (800-824-8000 in California).

Take Care of Her for Us

by Marjorie Holmes

The vet says there's nothing more he can do for her, God, she's better off home with us. I'm sitting with her now, holding her paw and wondering if she'll live till morning.

Your stars are shining through the window and pretty soon the moon will be bright. My father keeps telling me to come to bed, but I want her to know I'm near, Lord. I can't leave her to die alone. (She would never leave one of *us!*)

You know how faithful she always was, running to meet us after school, tagging us places, challenging anybody she thought might harm us. Oh, God, thank you for her—and forgive me for the times I failed her.

The times I forgot to feed her or was too lazy to walk her even when she begged. The times when she messed up my room or upset the trash and I was so cross with her. My heart breaks to think of it; the tears roll down my cheeks.

Please let her know I'm sorry.

She strives feebly with her paw and I hold it tighter, gaze into her poor pleading eyes. Her tail moves a little and I think she's trying to tell me something . . .

Oh, God, how sad to be dumb, unable to speak, to say words of forgiveness or love. Or even one word—"*Goodbye.*"

Where is she going, God? Do pets have souls like us?

Dogs, so eager to please, so loving, so loyal—do you have a place for them somewhere out there among the stars? A place where they can run and bark to their hearts' content, and love again—maybe love the angels? She never really cared about anybody but us, Lord, but don't let her get too lonesome. Don't let her miss us too much.

Please, Lord, if it's in your scheme of all, take care of her for us. And when the rest of us arrive, let her come bounding to meet us.

—from *Nobody Else Will Listen*, a book of prayers for teenage girls

A Prayer for Animals

Hear our humble prayer, O God, for our friends the animals, especially for animals who are suffering; for any that are hunted or lost or deserted or frightened or hungry; for all that must be put to death. We entreat for them all Thy mercy and pity, and for those who deal with them we ask a heart of compassion and gentle hands and kindly words. Make us ourselves to be true friends to animals and so to share the blessings of the merciful. Amen.

—Dr. Albert Schweitzer

For every beast of the forest is mine, and the cattle upon a thousand hills. I know all the fowls of the mountains: and the wild beasts of the field are mine.

—Psalms 50:10, 11

Acknowledgments

The author and Fleming H. Revell Company thank the following authors, publishers, and agents whose cooperation and permission to reprint have made possible the preparation of this book. All possible care has been taken to trace the ownership of every selection included and to make full acknowledgment for its use. If any errors have accidentally occurred, they will be corrected in subsequent editions, provided notification is sent to the publishers.

"A Man and His Animals" from *Straight Talk to Men and Their Wives* by James Dobson, copyright © 1980; used by permission of the author and of Word Books, Waco, Texas.

"How Our Dog Taught Me to Fetch" by Maynard Good Stoddard, reprinted with permission from *The Saturday Evening Post* Society, a division of BFL&MS, Inc., copyright © 1964.

"Little Dog Found" by Aletha Jane Lindstrom, reprinted with permission from *Guideposts* magazine. Copyright © 1987 by Guideposts Associates, Inc., Carmel, N.Y. 10512.

"Belle" by Marjorie Holmes, reprinted with permission from *Guideposts* magazine. Copyright © 1976 by Guideposts Associates, Inc., Carmel, N.Y. 10512.

"The Power of a Dog" by Rudyard Kipling, reprinted from *Rudyard Kipling's Verse—Inclusive Edition, 1885–1918*, copyright © 1918. Used with the permission of Doubleday & Company.

"The Legendary Hachiko" reprinted with permission of Macmillan Publishing Company from *Animal Heroes* by Byron G. Weis. copyright © 1979 by Laurence Gadd.

"Only a Dog" (Epitaph) reprinted with permission of Macmillan Publishing Company from *Animal Heroes* by Byron G. Weis. Copyright © 1979 by Laurence Gadd.

Information for "A Dog by Any Other Name . . ." item was supplied by Anderson Animal Shelter in South Elgin, Illinois. Used by permission.

"Half a Dog High" by Byron K. Elliott, reprinted with the permission of *The Saturday Evening Post* Society, a division of BFL&MS, Inc., copyright © 1986.

"I Just Want Kate to Get Well" by Phyllis Hobe, reprinted with permission from *Guideposts* magazine. Copyright © 1987 by Guideposts Associates, Inc., Carmel, N.Y. 10512.

Illustration on page 27 is a rubber stamp © All Night Media, Inc., San Anselmo, CA 94960. Stamp drawing by Robert Bloomberg. Used by permission.

Illustration on page 115 is a rubber stamp © 1988 by Marks of Distinction, Chicago, IL 60615. Used by permission.

Who loves me, let him love my dog also.
—St. Bernard

The author would enjoy hearing from readers with their own animal stories and photos. She regrets that the volume of mail may make it impossible for her to return photos or acknowledge correspondence. She may be addressed at P.O. Box 19822, Sacramento, CA 95819-0822.